Social Development Activities for Circle Time:
Getting Along

Ages 3-6

by
Patricia McFadden

Published by Totline® Publications
an imprint of
Frank Schaffer Publications®

Author: Patricia McFadden
Editor: Mary Rose Hassinger
Interior Designer: Good Neighbor Press, Inc.

Frank Schaffer Publications®

Totline Publications is an imprint of Frank Schaffer Publications.

Send all inquiries to:
Frank Schaffer Publications
8720 Orion Place
Columbus, Ohio 43240-2111

Social Development Activities for Circle Time: Getting Along—Ages 3–6

ISBN: 1-57029-526-3

2 3 4 5 6 7 8 9 10 PAT 10 09 08

Table of Contents

Table of Contents

Introduction

 ## A Note for Teachers

The most important teaching tool for "getting along" is you. The more gentle, soft-spoken, and patient you can be (and it's not easy, I know, when so many young ones are clamoring for your time, attention, and affection), the more your classroom will reflect these qualities. Children respond to kindness much as flowers respond to sunshine. It helps them grow and become strong enough to withstand harsh winds. Model "getting along" behavior, use the activities in this book, and expect the best of your students. Most of all, be the kind of person you hope your students will become, and chances are they will.

 ## Making the Most of Circle Time

Circle time is an invaluable part of the early childhood curriculum. Given that teaching small children is somewhat akin to herding chickens, circle time is often the only opportunity for getting your whole class together, on more or less the same page, during the day. This is where questions are answered, songs are sung, books read, games played, new concepts are introduced, and new behaviors practiced. It is a vital part of students' socialization process. It can also be one of the most frustrating activities for teachers. (Ever try to get chickens to sit in a circle?) Relax and try not to get upset if things don't go exactly as planned. If half a story is all your children can sit still for today, accept that it's a wiggly day and spend some extra time on the playground. If it's a (rare) laid-back day and everyone is reluctant to leave the circle, add another activity.

Younger children have a short attention span, usually not more than four or five minutes per activity, and no more than two or three activities per circle time. Older children have a lot more ability to sit still and stay

Introduction (continued)

interested, but even they tend to get restless after about 15 minutes or so. Many activities can be started in the circle and completed back in the open classroom. You can also have extensions, such as an art project that relates to a circle time activity.

Circle time isn't every child's cup of tea, nor is it reasonable to require every child to participate, but it *is* reasonable to expect the children who are not participating to be respectful of those who are. If you have several children who are recalcitrant circlers, it would be wise to have a space, well away from the circle area, where they may play quietly while circle time is going on. Make it clear that they are, of course, welcome to change their minds at any time and join the circle. My experience is that most, and usually all, of the nay-sayers at the beginning of the year eventually become "circle time converts" *if* you don't make a big deal out of it. Even the children who continue to stay away and seem to be paying no attention, are absorbing much more than you—or they—are aware of.

Children learn best when they are neither hungry nor tired. Therefore, having circle time right before either lunch or nap time is inadvisable. The best time to have circle activities is, in my experience, very soon after snacks. If you have a half-day program, one circle time is ample. In all-day programs, a second circle right before the children get picked up is nice for touching base and talking about how the day went for everyone. If someone had a particularly hard time with sharing that day, for example, you can do some role-playing while the incident is fresh in everyone's minds. This is also a good time to remind children of any special plans for the next day and to bring a sense of closure. Keep this circle time short, ending with a "see you tomorrow" song or chant.

Introduction (continued)

Establishing a circle routine is crucial. It is much easier to introduce new topics and concepts within a familiar framework. Give the children ample warning before circle time begins, and establish whatever ground rules are necessary—such as whether interrupted projects can be left out or should be put away for circle time, etc. Whatever pattern you follow—for example: opening activity; song or chant; story or game; closing activity—stick to it, especially the opening and closing activities. Otherwise, aim for variety. Songs and chants can be quiet or loud and involve lots of movement or none, stories can be told with big books, puppets, flannel board or dry-erase board, games can run the gamut from beanbag tosses to relays. Above all, HAVE FUN and your students will, too.

Fair Warning

It can be challenging to get children to drop what they're doing and come to circle time. Here are some ideas for giving them "fair warning" and easing them into joining the circle.

Circle Timer

Have a timer with a nice loud ring and warn children when you are setting it for circle time. Set the timer for five minutes and challenge children to "beat the clock." Encourage children to help each other put away toys, clean up art supplies and get to the circle. When the timer rings, do a 10-9-8- . . . countdown for the last few children.

My Spot

Using the pattern on page 9, make each child a "circle spot" with either green or purple paper. Let the children decorate their "spots" with stickers, stamps, markers, glitter, etc. Laminate the circles and have the children sit on their "spots" during circle time.

Extension: After laminating the "spots," punch holes around the edges and let each child "sew" around her spot with a shoelace or piece of yarn.

Ready Song

With all the children standing, begin by singing this song to the tune of "If You're Happy and You Know It." Switch the verses from day to day so that each group gets a turn to sit down first.

When you're ready for our circle, clap your hands (clap, clap).
When you're ready for our circle, clap your hands (clap, clap).
When you're ready for our circle, sit on your spot of purple
    (children with purple spots sit down).
When you're ready for our circle, clap your hands (clap, clap).

When you're ready to begin, clap your hands (clap, clap).
When you're ready to begin, clap your hands (clap, clap).
When you're ready to begin, sit on your spot of green
    (children with green spots sit down).
When you're ready to begin, clap your hands (clap, clap).

My Spot Reproducible

Directions: Fold large sheets of purple or green construction paper in half. Using the pattern below, cut a circle for each child in your class, divided evenly between the colors. Print the words *(Name of child)'s Circle Spot* on the circle. Let children decorate their circles. Laminate them and use them to define their seating area at circle time.

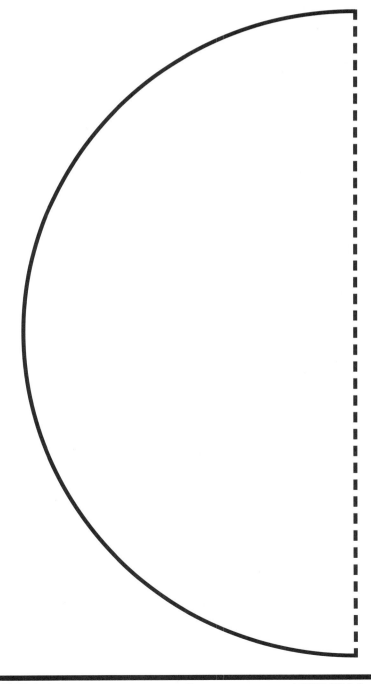

Gathering Together

Here are some alternative activities for starting your circle time. Do them instead of, or in addition to, the "When You're Ready . . ." song.

 ## "Marching 'Round the Circle" Song

(Sing to the tune of "Here We Go 'Round the Mulberry Bush.")

Here we go marching around our circle,
Around our circle, Around our circle
Here we go marching around our circle
All on a (day of the week) morning.

Here we go hopping around our circle,
Around our circle, Around our circle
Here we go hopping around our circle
All on a (day of the week) morning.

Here we go tiptoeing around our circle, etc.
Around our circle, Around our circle
Here we go tiptoeing around our circle
All on a (day of the week) morning.

Extension: Invite students to make up a verse. (galloping, walking backwards, skipping, crawling, etc.)

 ## "Happy to See You" Song

(Sing to the tune of "Dear, Dear, What Can the Matter Be.")

Hello, we're happy to see you,
Hello, we're happy to see you,
Hello, we're happy to see you,
Welcome to circle, (child's name).

Continue singing until everyone in the group has been greeted by name.

Hands Up Chant

This is a great way to get the last few wiggles out before getting down to business. Do the actions, seated, while you say the chant.

My hands go up	*Stretch arms up.*
My hands go down	*Put arms out with palms facing down.*
My hands make a square	*Touch tip of thumbs and forefingers.*
My hands are round	*Clasp hands into ball shape.*
My hands give a very loud clap!	*Clap hands once.*
My hands lay quietly in my lap.	*Lay hands in lap.*

Who's Got News?

Instead of show-and-tell, try this activity. Get a billed cap (paint stores often have them for free) and write *NEWS* on the bill with a marker. Show the children this news hat and explain that all get to take turns being the class news reporter. (Stress that this means good news, like a visit from Grandma.) Put the hat on and model reporting an interesting piece of good news from your own life. "Hello, this is Ms. Pat of Valley Pre-School, reporting that my cat just had kittens!" Once they have the idea, every so often, at the beginning of circle time, hold up the hat and ask, "Who's got news?" Call on two or three of the children whose hands are up. (This is a good time to practice hand-raising instead of shouting.) Invite them to take turns putting on the hat and reporting their news.

Extensions: Get an old microphone for the reporter to use.

You can also make individual microphones by covering toilet paper tubes with foil and gluing Styrofoam™ balls to the end of the tubes.

Keep a list of all the "news stories" and, every so often, publish a newspaper for parents.

Getting Started

Circle time can be viewed as the "business meeting" of the pre-school day. Here are some of the business matters you may wish to include in your meeting.

Weather Wise

It's very nice to have some framework for discussing the weather. Here are some suggestions for interesting ways to approach this subject. Have children take turns being the "weather person" for the day.

◆ Get or make a clock-face style weather chart with an arrow for the weather person to turn to indicate the weather. The usual categories are sunny, cloudy, windy, rainy, and snowy. Adjust for your local climate. For example, if you live somewhere that it seldom or never snows, but is often foggy, leave out snowy and add foggy. A pizza box liner makes a good base for this. Or children can make individual charts with paper plates and magazine pictures.

◆ Have a stuffed animal, such as a bear, with a variety of clothing options and invite the weather person to dress it for the current weather.

◆ Invite the weather person to put an appropriate sticker (raindrop, snowflake, sun, etc.) on the class calendar.

◆ Attach small paper plates to craft sticks. Draw or paste a picture of a different weather condition on each. Invite your weather person for the day to select the appropriate plate and stick it into a small flowerpot filled with sand.

◆ Have a prop box with a rain hat, pair of sunglasses, a windbreaker, and a pair of mittens. Invite the weather person to select and don the appropriate item of clothing for the day.

Chore Cups

At circle time, discuss what chores need to be done around the classroom. From the list you come up with, decorate a cup for each classroom chore, with both the name of the chore and picture that symbolizes the chore, for the pre-readers, on the side. Put the cups on a windowsill or glue them to a piece of poster board mounted on the wall. Include an extra cup at each end, one marked *Chore Sticks* and one marked *Done*. Follow the directions on page 65 to make chore sticks and use as described.

 # Song Board

Using a colorful poster board, divide it with a ruler and marker into ten to twelve sections. Draw or find pictures to illustrate favorite class songs (such as the picture of a duck for "Five Little Ducks.") Put a different picture in each section. You may want to leave some blank sections at first so you can add to your song board as the year progresses. Invite one of the children to be the "song selector" of the day. Have him go to the board, point to the song he would like to sing, and lead the singing.

Extension: You can do a similar activity with Mother Goose rhymes or fairy stories.

Five Little Ducks	Twinkle, Twinkle, Little Star	Five Little Monkeys	Itsy Bitsy Spider
BINGO	I Had a Little Turtle	ABCs	Teddy Bear, Teddy Bear
The Wheels on the Bus	London Bridge	Ring Around the Rosey	Three Blind Mice

 # Super Stretches

After taking care of business, you and your students will probably be ready for a good, long s-t-r-e-t-c-h. Here's a chant to help you get the kinks out.

I stand on tiptoe like a crane.	*Stand on tiptoe and stretch arms straight up.*
I stretch my wings out like a plane.	*Spread arms out to side.*
I lean to the sides like a crescent moon.	*Arms over head, hands touching, lean left then right.*
I bend my 'til my back's round as a balloon.	*Bend over, try to touch toes.*
I stand up straight, as straight can be.	*Stand up, arms at side.*
I am so glad that I am me.	*Wrap arms around self, hug.*

Circle Rules

Learning to follow rules is part of the "getting along" process. Here are some suggestions for making your circle time run smoothly.

"Sitting on the Line" Song

Sing this to the tune of "Ring Around the Rosey" when little bottoms start to scoot and little bodies start to sprawl.

We're sitting on the line.
We're sitting here just fine.
Ears open, mouths closed,
We sit up STRAIGHT.

Talking Bear

Using the reproducible on page 15, color, cut out, and laminate the "Talking Bear." Show the bear to your students and explain that he is a very special talking bear, like the talking sticks that some Native Americans use in their powwows. When someone holds the talking bear, she is the only one who may speak. Everyone else's job is to listen. Emphasize how important it is to really listen to each other. Practice using the talking bear by asking a simple question, such as, "What is your favorite animal?" and passing the talking bear around, making sure that everyone has a chance to answer. Use the talking bear for group discussions of all sorts.

Extension: Make copies of "Talking Bear" on tagboard for each student to color and cut out. Send them home with a brief explanation of the concept for parents.

"Talking Bear" Poem

Read your students this poem to help them remember the rules for the talking bear.

When I hold the talking bear
I get to have my say.
While everybody listens
That's the talking bear way.
When you have the talking bear
I'll be quiet and listen to you,
With ears open and mouth closed
So you get to have your say, too.

Talking Bear Reproducible

Copy the pattern below on tagboard, color, cut out, and laminate. Use during circle time to help students with listening skills.

All Together Now

This is a variation of follow-the-leader that helps children learn to be part of the group. The first time you do this, start with a mirroring exercise. Choose a child and have her sit in front of you. Explain that you are going to do whatever she does, just as though you were her mirror. After the two of you have done a few gestures, invite the children to pair off and try this exercise themselves. The next circle time, remind the children of the mirroring exercise and tell them that now that they know how to be mirrors, everyone is going to do it together. Go around the circle and invite each child to think of a movement that everyone else copies. Keep going until everyone has had a turn at being the leader.

Extensions: With older children, challenge each successive child to repeat all the prior gestures before adding one of his own.

Challenge children to think of an animal and make a gesture which indicates that animal. The other children have to guess the animal before repeating the gesture.

"Wiggle Worms" Song

Sometimes children just can't sit still. If they are having a particularly wiggly day, relax, bow to the inevitable, and teach them this song.

Invite all the children to lie on their tummies on the circle line, facing in. As they sing, they wiggle into the center and back out again. Sing to the tune of "We Are Climbing Jacob's Ladder."

We are wiggling into the circle,
We are wiggling into the circle,
We are wiggling into the circle,
We are wiggly worms.

We are wiggling out of the circle,
We are wiggling out of the circle,
We are wiggling out of the circle,
We are wiggly worms.

Ending the Circle

Having some sort of ending routine for circle helps eliminate the mad rush. Here are some circle-ending ideas for you to try.

"The Circle Is Open" Song

This chant is adapted from an old Celtic tradition. Hold hands and walk around the circle while singing the following to the tune of "London Bridge."

Our circle is now open, open, open
When next we have our circle,
We'll be peaceful.

All Those Wearing Pink . . .

A good way to dismiss the circle is to break it up gradually by dividing the group into smaller units, such as: "Everyone wearing pink may now leave the circle. Everyone wearing green may now leave the circle, etc." Colors are generally easiest, but you can use all sorts of divisions: color of hair, types of shoes, everyone with a little brother or sister, people whose names start with a certain letter of the alphabet, etc. You can also designate destinations, such as "Tommy, Sally, and Ben may go to the water table, George, Allen, and Ken may finish your block tower, etc." This works well if children were interrupted in the middle of a project that they want to continue.

"So Long" Song

(Sing to the tune of "Oh Dear, What Can the Matter Be?") This is a good song for an afternoon circle time.

So long, we'll see you on (next day of class),
So long, we'll see you on (next day of class),
So long, we'll see you on (next day of class),
And we'll have lots more fun!

 # Bye, Bye, Bunny Hop

Play some lively music at the end of circle and teach the children to Bunny Hop to the next activity. Once everyone is standing up, invite them to turn to the side and hold onto the waist of the child in front. You get to be the leader the first time. Once they know the steps, invite different children to lead. First, stick your left foot out twice, then your right foot out twice, then hop backwards once and forward twice. Repeat. That's all there is to it. Lead the group away from the circle, either around the room or out to the playground.

 # "Aloha" Song

In Hawaiian, *Aloha* means both "hello" and "good-bye." Sing this song to the tune of "Aloha Oi." Teach students some simple hula movements to go along with the song.

Aloha, friends	*Do hula wave to the left.*
Aloha, friends	*Do hula wave to the right.*
Our circle's at an end.	*Make a big circle with arms.* *Shake your head and look sad.*
Aloha, friends	*Hold right elbow with left hand and wave.*
Aloha, friends	*Hold left elbow with right hand and wave.*
Until we meet again.	*Turn around slowly, doing hula wave to left.* *Bow with hands together in front of chest.*

 # Reminder Slips

Use the form below to make a reminder slip for children to take home to parents. A good way to end circle is to hand the slips out one at a time, and give each child a moment to put his slip in his cubby before dismissing the next child.

- -

Child's Name _____ Date _____

In school tomorrow we will _____.

Please be sure to bring: _____

Your classroom will be a friendlier place if you take some time to get to know each other better during circle time.

Who Are We?

Circle time is a great place for your students and you to learn new things about each other. Here are some activities for getting better acquainted.

Name Clapping

On your first day, go around the circle and find out children's whole names—first, middle, and last. Most children know all their names, but be sure you have a list for the rare child who doesn't. Say each name together, clapping once for each syllable. For example: Su *(clap)* sie *(clap)* May *(clap)* Hol *(clap)* is *(clap)* ter *(clap)*. Say each name three times, increasing the speed of the clapping each time. After you've clapped for everyone's names, give yourselves a final round of applause.

Extensions: Use rhythm sticks instead of clapping.

Ring jingle bells instead of clapping.

Stand up and stomp instead of clapping.

Pet Chart

Using a large piece of paper or poster board, make a chart with the children's names on lines down the side and pictures of various kinds of pets in columns across the top. Invite each child to go to the chart and put red dot stickers on the chart for each of their pets. Encourage them to tell the other students something about their pet(s). For children who don't have a pet, let them put a blue dot sticker for the kind of pet they'd like to have, and tell why they want it. Lead into a discussion about responsibility by asking what the children do to help take care of their pets.

Extensions: This kind of chart can be used for all sorts of subjects such as favorite food, favorite color, number of people in students' families, etc.

To increase pre-math skills, count together how many spots are in each column and write the tallies across the bottom.

 # Colorful Circle

This is another group game with color recognition. Ask all the students wearing green to stand up. Then ask all the children wearing red to stand up. By the time you get through the entire color list, all the children will be standing. This is a good lead-in to an ending activity.

Extensions: Instead of standing up, invite students to make a different gesture for each color, such as: "Wrinkle your nose if you are wearing blue; pat your tummy if you are wearing red; scratch your head if you are wearing pink; etc."

Ask children, to hold up a finger for every color that they're wearing. After calling out all the colors, go round the circle and invite each child to count their fingers and say how many colors they're wearing.

 # Introducing . . .

This is another good getting-acquainted exercise. Explain that you're going to go around the circle, and each person will get a chance to tell their favorite (whatever category you choose). Emphasize that they need to listen very carefully, because, once everyone has had a turn, you'll go around the circle again and introduce each other. Start by saying, "My name is (your name) and my favorite food is (whatever)." Once you've gotten all the way around, go to one of the children, lead her into the center of the circle, and say, "I'd like to introduce my friend. This is (child's name) and her favorite food is (whatever)." You sit down and the child you introduced chooses another child to introduce. Continue until all the children have been introduced.

Extension: Have each child choose an animal that they'd like to be. Get a top hat for the introducer. Make the introductions in the style of a circus announcer: "Ladies and gentlemen! Introducing, in the center ring, Sarah the chimpanzee!" The child being introduced then chatters or roars, or whatever is appropriate for the animal she picked. They then get to be the introducer.

Special Us

"Many Friends" Poem

Read this poem to your students during circle. At art time, copy the blank face on page 22 and invite children to use it to draw a picture of one of their friends. At the next circle time, share the pictures and discuss them.

Many Friends

I have friends both near and far.
Some friends I visit in a car.
Some friends live in my neighborhood.
Having many friends feels good.

All the friends I see at school
Are lots of fun and very cool.
We play with blocks and sand and clay.
I get to see them every day.

I have friends both old and new.
I'm happy that I'm friends with YOU!

Life-Size Paper Dolls

In the center of the circle, have each child lie down on a sheet of butcher paper and trace around her. Invite children to say the following chant and clap their hands while waiting their turn to be traced. At art time, invite your students to finish their dolls and cut them out. Display on the walls.

Paper Doll Chant

Fee, fi, fo, foll
We get to see a paper doll
That's just as short and just as tall
As (child's name) and that is all.

Extension: Have ribbon, buttons, and yarn for hair to make dolls more 3-D.

My Friend Reproducible

This is my friend, _____.

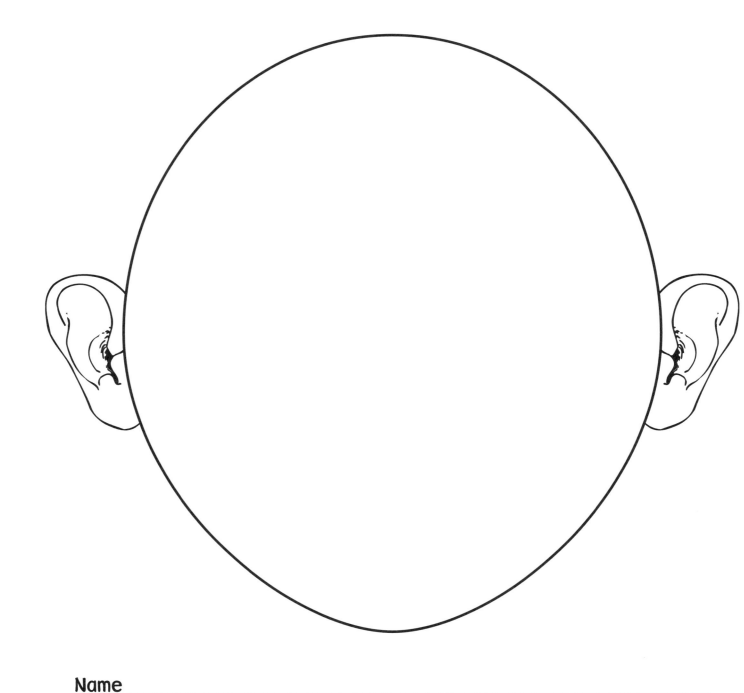

Name _____

Everybody's Special Chant

Using the talking bear (page 15), go around the circle and invite children to think of something special about themselves. Once everyone has thought of something, teach them this chant and say it for each child.

Everybody's special.
I know that this is true.
I'm a special me.
And you're a special you.

(Child's name) is special.
In a very special way.
He/She (name the special thing the child thought of)
Hip! Hip! Hooray!

Extension: Invite students to think of something special about one of their classmates.

Daily Special

At restaurants, they often list a "daily special." This is an item that is special because it's only on the menu for one day. Acknowledge an individual child each day by declaring her the daily special. Decide ahead of time what privilege(s) the daily special gets, such as being first in line for the playground, or first at show-and-tell. If parents provide snacks, the daily special could be the child who brings the snack that day. Announce the daily special at circle time. Make sure all the children get a turn to be special for a day.

Extension: Include a daily special spot on your class bulletin board and post a picture of the daily special child there.

Special School Mural

Before circle time, put a long piece of butcher paper on the wall, at the right height for the children. Across the top, write *We Are Special*. During circle time, talk about ways that your school or class is special. As children come up with suggestions, write them on the bottom of the paper. For an art activity, invite students to work together on a mural to illustrate their words.

Expanding the Circle

Circle time is ideal for inviting people into your class, and expanding your students' knowledge of and appreciation for all sorts of interesting folks.

Getting Along with Nature

Young children are very interested in the natural world. Here are some suggestions for helping them develop a sense of connection with, and responsibility for, our beautiful home.

✦ Check with local gardening clubs and ask if one of their members would come talk to your class—and maybe even help you start a class garden.

✦ There are all sorts of nature appreciation clubs. Bird-watchers, wildflower spotters, conservationists, and others are always happy to talk about their passion.

✦ Contact the local recycling plant and ask them to send someone to your class to talk to your students about recycling.

Getting Along in Our Community

There are a lot of people in every community who help out. Firemen and policemen immediately come to mind. However, there are a lot of other, less recognized contributors to community well-being that your students would enjoy meeting. For instance:

✦ Where does the trash go when it is picked up, and what happens after you flush the toilet? Why not invite a trash collector or sewage treatment engineer to class to talk about their jobs?

✦ When snow starts falling, who gets up at three a.m. to plow the roads? Ask your local road maintenance department, and see if one of their snowplow drivers would be willing to visit your class. He may even bring his snowplow for your students to see up close and personal.

✦ Encourage your students to notice the community helpers all around them. Make a class collage or put together a class book of people whom they've observed being community helpers.

Invite a Family Member to Class

Set aside a day for students to bring a family member to class. Invite children to introduce their family members at circle time and give the class a chance to find out a little bit about each one. Take photos of students and their family member and post them on the bulletin board. Encourage children to ask grandparents, aunts, uncles, and cousins, as well as members of their immediate family.

Extensions: Have a specific day for different family members, such as a grandparents day, a brother/sister day, a cousin day, etc.

Have a "When I Was a Baby" Day. Invite students to bring in pictures of themselves when they were babies. At circle time, pass the pictures around and discuss the ways babies have for communicating and "getting along" (smiling, clapping, kissing and hugging, laughing, etc.). Encourage students to list more ways they have learned to get along, now that they are bigger.

"Pets Are Our Friends, Too" Song

(Sing to the tune of "The Farmer In the Dell.")
Sing this song to remind students that animals deserve to be treated kindly, too.

Pets are our friends, too.
Pets are our friends, too.
Cats and dogs
And spotted frogs
Pets are our friends, too.

We take care of our pets.
We take care of our pets.
We give them food
And lots of love
We take care of our pets.

Extension: Invite children to bring in pictures of their pets to share at circle time. For children who don't have pets, have some magazines with pet pictures and invite them to find or draw a picture of the kind of pet they'd like to have.

Everybody's Different, Everyone's the Same

Help your students learn to celebrate their differences and also recognize and enjoy their similarities with these circle time activities.

Individual and Unique Cheer

Young children adore learning great big words. Here are two one-of-a-kind words to add to their vocabulary. Stand up and do it like a cheering squad would.

There's no one else like me.	*Point to yourself, shake head.*
I'm an in-div-id-u-al.	*Clap for each beat.*
There's no one else like you.	*Point to another person, shake head.*
You are to-tall-y u-nique.	*Clap for each beat.*
Ev-e-ry-bo-dy is one-of-a-kind.	*Clap for each beat.*
That's how it should be. YAY!	*Lift both arms, like signaling a touchdown, and jump up and down.*

"Being Different" Poem

Read this poem to your students and invite them to act it out.

Hooray for being different!
How silly it would be
If I were just like you,
And you were just like me.
I'd scratch when you had chickenpox.
At school, we'd wear each other's socks.
Your mom would take me to your home.
My friends would call you on my phone.
I'd blow your birthday candles out.
You'd get my gifts! There is no doubt,
As anyone can plainly see,
Different is the way to be.

Diversity Circle

Using the talking bear, go around the circle and invite your students to think of something special and unique about themselves. Then go around again and invite each student to think of something special and unique about the person sitting next to her or him.

Extension: As students talk, write their observations on a separate sheet of paper for each person. At art time, invite students to draw a picture of their unique selves.

All the Colors of the Rainbow

At circle time, have some sheets of construction paper in several colors, and a book with colorful pictures. Hold the paper up, one sheet at a time, and ask the children to name the color. Once you've done some color recognition, ask the children: "Are these blank pieces of paper very interesting? Why?" Now look at the pictures in the book. Ask: "Are the pictures more interesting than the blank paper? Why?" Point out that it takes many colors to make a picture, not just one, just like it takes many kinds of people and animals and plants to make the world.

"Rainbow" Song

(Sing to the tune of "Mary Had a Little Lamb.")
Teach your students this song to help them learn to celebrate their differences.

Every single rainbow, rainbow, rainbow
Has red and purple, yellow, blue,
Orange and brilliant green.

Without these different colors, colors, colors
These lovely, special colors
No rainbow could be seen.

Because we are all different, different, different
The world's the biggest rainbow
That there has ever been.

 # Top to Toe Similarities Chant

Standing on the circle, invite everyone to say the following chant while touching the appropriate parts of their body. On the last line, shake hands with the person next to you.

Lots of hair

upon my head,

Two ears,

Two eyes,

One mouth to be fed.

Shoulders,

Tummy,

Knees and feet,

Same parts on

Everyone you meet.

 # Fee, Fi, Fo, Feeling Game

Everyone has the same feelings, and expresses them in much the same way. To help your students understand this concept, introduce this game at circle time. Start by discussing some common feelings, such as happy, sad, angry, sleepy, etc. Invite students to take turns thinking of a feeling and acting it out. Have them begin by saying, "Fee, Fi, Fo, what am I feeling?" then smile, frown, or whatever. For very young children, you might want to do the acting out, keeping it very simple, and let them do the guessing. After the game, start a discussion. Point out that everyone's feelings seem to be a lot alike. Ask, "Is it good that everyone feels many of the same things? Why?"

 # Everyone Needs

Start this circle activity by saying, "Everyone's a lot alike. Everyone needs food." Encourage the child next to you to repeat what you said and then add an item. She'd say, "Everyone's a lot alike. Everyone needs food and clothes." Keep going around the circle, with each child adding something that everyone needs. Encourage them to think of intangible as well as tangible things, such as love, happiness, etc.

 # All in the Family

Children often hear that they have ears just like their father, or a little toe just like Aunt Jane. Start a circle discussion about the way families share characteristics. Challenge students to list a way they are like someone in their family.

Extension: For an art project, invite children to draw a picture of the family member they look the most like.

 # Lots of Groups

Even small children know that some people get treated poorly because they are part of a certain group. Show your students how silly such prejudice is by doing this circle time activity. Challenge your students to see how many different ways they can group themselves. For example, how about a group of everyone with curly hair, or everyone who's ridden an airplane? Be creative. Who's in the left-handed group? Who has the same middle initial? Who's in the group that shares a room with a sibling? How about a group of children who can stand on one leg and cross their eyes? Encourage children to think of more categories, the kookier the better. Point out that everyone belongs to lots of different groups, not just one, and it's silly to judge someone on the basis of any one group they happen to be part of.

 # "Short to Tall" Song

Help students sort themselves out from short to tall. When you get them lined up, hold hands and march around the circle singing this song to the tune of "Twinkle, Twinkle, Little Star."

Tall to short, and short to tall
Our circle holds us, one and all.
We're each different, yes it's true,
Different me and different you.
But, when with hearts
And hands we meet
We all march
To the very same beat.

Friendly Books

Read some of these books to your students at story time, to encourage friendly discussions.

Oliver's High Five by Beverly Swerdlow Brow and Margot J. Ott, (Heath Press, 1997)
Oliver has only five tentacles, instead of eight, but he proves that being different can be a very good thing.

Yoko and Friends by Rosemary Wells (Hyperion, 1998)
This is a story about being different, in this case bringing sushi for lunch, and how Yoko eventually comes to grips with being different without giving up her comfort food or her heritage.

Mr. George Baker by Amy Hest and Jon J. Muth (Candlewick, 2004)
Mr. George Baker is 100 years old. Harry is six. They ride the bus together every day because they are both learning to read, and they are friends.

Emily and Albert by Jan Ormerod and David Slonim (Chronicle Books, 2004)
Emily is an ostrich, Albert is an elephant. They are very good friends.

Handsigns: A Sign Language Alphabet by Kathlene Fain (Chronicle Books, 1993)
A very good and unusual introduction to sign language for young children.

House-Mouse Friends by Ellen Jareckie (Little, Brown and Company, 2004)
All the House-Mouse stories by Ellen Jareckie are charming. This one is about the mice befriending all sorts of other animals, even a penguin.

The Useful Moose: A Truthful, Mooseful Tale by Fiona Robinson (Abrams Books, 2004)
A funny story about a little girl named Molly and three funny moose whom she befriends.

Using Good Words

"Bee" Positive

Using the reproducible on page 32, make a bee for each child. Invite children to color the bees and cut them out. During circle time, discuss the difference between "sweet" or positive words, such as *thank you, I like you, good job* and "bitter" or negative words such as *you're stupid, I don't like you, go away.* Ask: "How does it make you feel when someone says sweet words to you? How does it make you feel when someone says bitter words to you?" Help each child think of some sweet words to write on her bee. Once everyone's bee is done, go around the circle, and have each child hold up their bee and say their sweet words.

Extensions: Use the completed bees to make a bulletin board.

Make a list of all the good words the children came up with and send a copy home with each child.

Get some bee stickers and award one to any student you hear using positive words.

Bitter Words "Bee" Gone

If a lot more bitter than sweet words seem to be flying around your classroom, try this circle time activity. Draw a picture of a beehive on the side of a large brown paper bag. Put all the bees from the last exercise in the bag. Have a stack of gray file cards or construction paper. Put the bag in the center of the circle. Tell the children that bees can take any kind of plant nectar, even from bitter plants like sage or buckwheat, and make sweet honey out of it. Invite children to think of some bitter words they've heard or used, and help write them on the gray papers. Then, invite children to take turns putting their bitter words in the hive and pulling out a bee with sweet words, instead.

Extension: Have some powdered sage or buckwheat flour, and a sample of honey from the same plant, for children to taste. (Check with parents for allergies before doing this.)

Positive Words Bee Reproducible

Color the bee and think of a sweet word for it to carry.

Thumbs Up!

Show students the "thumbs up" gesture. Explain to them that it started in ancient Rome. When two gladiators fought, the Roman Emperor gave the gladiator who lost either a "thumbs up," which meant "let him live" or a "thumbs down" which meant "kill him." Nowadays, however, we use the "thumbs up" gesture to show we think that someone has done a good job. Ask your children to think of a time when they did something that deserved a "thumbs up." If they have trouble thinking of something, prompt them a bit—"Remember when you helped Sally pick up all the blocks?" After they say what they did, have everyone else say "Thumbs up to (child's name)!" and make the thumbs up gesture. Once you are sure your students know what it means, continue to use the "thumbs up" gesture when one of them masters a new skill or does something else worthy of acknowledgment. Soon, they'll be giving each other "thumbs up."

Say It with "I"

Begin by discussing the difference between *I* messages, such as: *I feel sad when you tell me to go away*, and *you* messages, such as: *You're mean not to let me play with you*. Ask, *which message would make you change your mind about playing with someone? Which message says something about the person's feelings? Which message do you think is best? Why?* Invite children to come up with other instances where an *I* message would be more useful than a *you* message.

Extension: For an art project, invite students to decorate large, cardboard *I* shapes. Make a bulletin board display with them, and encourage children to remind each other to *say it with "I."*

Mind Your Manners

Having good manners helps everyone get along better. Here are some manner-minding circle activities to try.

Excuse Me Game

This game is a variation of Red Rover. Have a discussion about manners in general and the fact that it's polite to say "excuse me" when you need to get past someone. Then play this game. Divide into two teams, one on each side of the circle. Each team holds hands. One side begins by saying, "Red Rover, Red Rover, send (child from other team) over." That child walks to the other side and says, "Excuse me" to two students. They make a space and the child gets between them and takes their hands. Then the other team calls someone over, and so on, until all the students have changed sides.

"Please" and "Thank You" Game

Have a basket of erasers, or other small objects that students may keep, one per child. Start a discussion about manners and using polite words such as *please* and *thank you*. Ask, "How do you feel when someone is rude and grabs without asking, or doesn't say 'thank you' when you give them something?" After the discussion, bring out the basket and explain that this is a manners game, and you will start. Hold out the basket to the student to your right and say, "Would you like an eraser? Prompt the student to say, "Yes, please," take an eraser out of the basket, and say "Thank you." You say, "You're welcome" and hand him the basket. He then turns to the student on his right and offers her an eraser. Continue around the circle, reminding students if they forget the proper words to use.

"Manners" Song

(Sing to the tune of "Are You Sleeping?")

Please and thank you,
Please and thank you,
Excuse me,
Excuse me,
Manners are important!
Manners are important!
They help us get along
So let's sing our manners song.

Respect is crucial for getting along. *Respect* means "treating others as kindly, and with as much understanding, as we would like to be treated." Children feel safest when they know that respect for their feelings, bodies, and environment is something that they will both receive and be expected to give in the classroom.

Respect for Each Other's Feelings

Feelings matter. Words can sometimes hurt even worse than sticks and stones. Here are some ways to help children learn to be careful of each other's feelings.

Happy Face/Sad Face Plates

For each student, take two small paper plates and staple together with a craft stick in the middle, for a handle. At art time, help children draw a happy face on one side of their plates, and a sad face on the other side. At circle time, invite students to bring their plates. Talk about the fact that some words are good for our feelings and other words hurt our feelings.

Encourage children to hold up either their happy or sad face, depending on whether they consider a word hurtful or helpful.

Extensions: Invite students to pair off and role-play happy and sad exchanges, using their plates to illustrate their feelings. For example:

> Billy: *Go away, Sally. I don't like you.*
> Sally (holds up her sad face): *Ouch, that hurts. I am sad.*
> Billy: *I'm sorry, Sally. Let's be friends.*
> Sally (holds up her happy face): *That feels better. I am happy!*

Encourage children to think of real-life instances of words that have hurt their feelings and words that have made them feel good.

Make a list of "feel good" words and encourage children to use them. You could have a Good Word for the Day and challenge children to use it as many times as possible.

"Everyone Has Feelings" Song

(Sing to the tune of "Mary Had a Little Lamb.")

Everyone has feelings, feelings, feelings.
Everyone has feelings
Because we are alive.

Everyone is sad sometimes, glad sometimes, mad sometimes.
Everyone has feelings
Because we are alive.

Be careful of others' feelings, feelings, feelings.
Be careful of others' feelings
And everyone will thrive.

A-A-R-G-H!

Feelings aren't good or bad, they just are. Help your students learn how to express their feelings appropriately with this exercise. Standing on the circle, invite someone to think of a feeling, a sound that expresses that feeling, and an action to go with the feeling. For example: You might start the ball rolling by saying, "When I feel angry, it sounds like this: A-A-R-G-H! and it looks like this. (Stomp up and down.) Now you try it." (Everybody goes 'a-a-r-g-h,' and stomps.) Invite as many children as want to show a feeling. If they get stumped, make some suggestions, such as "What does it sound and look like when you're lonely? What does it sound and look like when you're excited? etc."

Just One of Those Days

Read *Alexander and the Terrible, Horrible, No Good, Very Bad Day* by Judith Viorst (Aladdin 1987). Start a discussion. "Have you ever had a really bad day? What happened? How did you feel? Did things get better? How did that feel? etc." Encourage children to brainstorm ideas for ways to help themselves and others feel better, especially when things aren't going well.

Compliment Kitty Game

Nothing's better feeling than getting a compliment. Play this game in circle time to make sure everybody gets their share of "strokes." Ask one child to be the "Compliment Kitty." She gets down on her hands and knees and, pretending to be a cat, goes up to another child and meows. That child pats her head and says, "Nice (child's name). I like (something about that child)." Everybody repeats the compliment and the compliment kitty purrs. The child she went to then becomes the compliment kitty and goes to another child for a compliment.

Pounding Pillow

Sometimes angry feelings just happen. Introduce the concept of a "pounding pillow" to your class at circle time. Start a discussion about feeling angry with such questions as, "When was the last time you felt really angry? What did you do? What happened then?" Emphasize that everyone has a right to all their feelings. It's not their feelings that need to be changed, just how they express them. Have a nice fat pillow. Show it to the class and tell them that this is their "official pounding pillow." Explain that when a person is angry it is not okay to hit others, or say bad words, or throw things (or whatever other unacceptable behaviors you may have been experiencing in the classroom) but it *is* okay to pound the pillow just as hard and long as they need to. Once they get used to it, you'll begin hearing "Just a minute, I need to go pound the pillow!" instead of tears and fights.

"Sticks and Stones" Poem

Teach your children this poem at circle time.

Sticks and stones
May break our bones
But words can hurt us, too.
The words you say
Stay in my heart
And my words stay with you.

So if you say
Nice words to me
And I say kind words to you,
Our hearts will glow
And we will know
That we're friends our whole life through.

Respect for Each Other's Bodies

Little ones can be rough with each other's bodies. Here are some ways to remind them to respect each other's "personal space."

 ## "Gently, Gently" Song

(Sing this song to the tune of "Row, Row, Row Your Boat.")

"Gent-ly, gent-ly,

That is how we touch.

When we're nice

With our friends

They like it very much."

 ## Body Language

Make some simple gestures such as shaking your finger and frowning, and waving and smiling. Ask the children to guess what you're trying say with your "body language." Have students come up with some gestures to use with each other, such as cupping their ear if they want someone to listen, or crossing their arms and/or holding out their hand in a "stop" gesture if they don't want someone to touch them.

 ## Personal Space Invaders Game

Using chalk or tape, before story time, make two concentric rings in the center of the circle, one 12 inches in diameter and one four feet in diameter. Talk about the way everyone has a "personal space" around them, and that it's important to respect each other's "personal spaces." Then play this game. Have one child stand in the center ring blindfolded while a second child stands somewhere on the outside ring. The second child then tries to creep as close as possible to the first child "without touching her." When the first child senses the second child, she goes "Woo, woo! Space Invader!" She then indicates where he is (in front of her, behind her, to the side, etc.). If she is right, the first child then sits down, the second child gets in the middle, and someone else becomes the "space invader." After playing the game, expect students to begin saying, "Woo, woo, space invader!" if someone invades their personal space.

Body Soccer Game

Use a Nerf™ or beach ball for this game. Invite children to sit on the circle with their legs spread out. Start by rolling the ball to one of the children and calling out a body part, such as "elbow" or "nose." The child catches the ball, then rolls it on to another child, using the body part named. The only rule is that no hands are allowed, just like in regular soccer. Before or after the game, discuss why you are using a soft ball for this game and emphasize the importance of being careful of each other's bodies no matter what game you're playing.

Gentle Pet Practice

A good way to learn gentleness is to practice with pets. Bring a stuffed animal to the circle, the more lifelike the better. Start a discussion about the best way to hold and handle pets. For instance, always support a cat's hind feet when you pick him up, and never pick any animal up by its neck. Demonstrate your talk with the stuffed animal. Pass one or more stuffed animals around and encourage children to practice gentle pet skills.

Extension: Ask someone from the Humane Society to visit your classroom and bring a puppy or kitten for the children to practice their gentle pet skills on.

Circle Back Rub

Encourage children to be kind to each other by doing this exercise. After sitting down in the circle, ask everyone to turn to the left and give the person in front of them a back rub. Everyone gets and gives a back rub at the same time. This is a good way to calm down the class if they have been particularly wild. Remind everyone to be gentle. Most children love this, but be sure it's clear that it's okay not to participate, as some children don't like to be touched.

Allow Me

To encourage positive physical interaction among your students, do this exercise. Have everyone bring a coat or sweater to the circle. Explain that lords and ladies have valets and maids to help them get dressed, so the class is going to take turns being "lords" and "ladies" and "valets" and "maids" by helping each other put on their outdoor wrap. Ask one of your students to pick up the next child's coat and hold it for her, saying "Allow me, my lady." The "lady" says, "Thank you, (child's name)" and puts the coat on. The "lady" then becomes a "maid" and helps the next child get his coat on, and so on around the circle. This is a good circle ending for transitioning to the playground.

Extension: Do the same thing for getting shoes, hats, and/or mittens on.

Encourage children to help each other whenever they are getting ready to go outside.

Elephant Walk

This is a funny activity that helps children with coordination while encouraging them to pay attention to each other's physical space. Have everyone stand on the circle. Explain that you are going to do an "elephant walk" around the circle. Each child leans over and reaches one hand behind them, between their legs. This is their "tail." They reach in front with their other hand. This is their "trunk." Each "elephant" holds the "tail" of the "elephant" in front of him with his "trunk." Put on some good marching music and walk around the circle, or use the following chant.

Extension: Challenge your "elephants" to skip, tiptoe, etc., without losing their grip.

Very young children may not have long enough arms to do this, so just have them reach behind with one arm and ahead with the other.

Elephant Chant

We're jolly elephants

Doing a circle dance.

We hold on tight,

With all our might,

As round and round we prance.

Respect for Each Other's Things

All of us have things that are important to us. Learning to respect other people's possessions is part of growing up.

Cubby Manners

It's important for students to respect each other's cubbies since they're the only personal space children have in the classroom. If you're having problems with this, start a circle discussion about cubby manners by asking such questions as: "Where do you put your belongings? When you put something in your cubby, how does it feel if someone takes it out without asking?" Help children think up some simple rules for cubby manners, write them up, and post them near the cubbies.

Extension: Have a Cubby Cleaning Day every so often, especially if things are falling out or getting mislaid. Invite children to go through their cubbies and put everything that needs to go home in a large bag. If you use paper bags for this, children can decorate them at art time and, hopefully, keep them to use throughout the year.

"My Things" Song

Sometimes small children don't want to share their things because they're afraid they won't get them back. Here's a song to help. Sing to the tune of "The Farmer in the Dell."

Some things belong to me,
Some things belong to you.
I get to say
who I let play
With my things, and so do you.

It's fun to play together
Inside and outdoors.
I'll let you play
With my toys today
If you let me play with yours.

Yours, Mine, and Ours Game

For circle time, invite children to bring something of their own that is easily recognizable. Going around the circle, give children some time to show their possessions to the circle and perhaps tell a little bit about them. Also, have the same number of items from around the classroom as there are children in the circle. Invite children to put their possessions in a large bag, along with the items from the classroom. Going around the circle, children take an item from the bag and identify it as "yours, mine, or ours." If the item is "yours," the child hands it to its owner. If it is "mine," she keeps it, and if it is "ours," she puts it back in its place in the classroom. Once the bag has gone around twice, all the items should be back where they belong.

Extension: Ask one of the children to cover her eyes. All the other children put their personal objects behind their backs, except one, who puts his object in the center of the circle. The child with her eyes closed then looks at the object and names who it belongs to. Or, have everyone keep their objects in their lap, except for one, who puts it behind his back. The child with her eyes closed then has to name the missing item. Either game is a good memory exercise.

Personal Beanbags

Lots of circle time activities can be done with beanbags. Making personal beanbags helps children with name recognition and also gives them a sense of ownership. Cut felt into 4" squares. At art time, give two squares to each child. Invite all the children to decorate their squares with rubber stamps and/or fabric paint. Write each child's name on one of her squares with an indelible marker or fabric paint. (Hint: Don't use puffy paint for this activity as it has a tendency to flake off.) Using a sewing machine, sew the squares together on three sides, or, if your students are old enough to do it by hand, invite them to sew three sides together. Put a handful of beans into each bag and invite the children to sew the remaining side shut. Even small children can manage to sew at least the fourth side, with a little help, and are very proud of their work. Use the beanbags in the circle activities on the next page.

Beanbag Games

The games listed below help with coordination, motor skills, cognitive thinking and, of course, getting along.

Beanbag Circle Walk

Invite children to put their beanbags on their heads and walk around the circle. Once everyone can get around the circle without their beanbag falling off, try some new things like walking backwards, skipping, and crawling. Invite children to think of some other ways to move.

Pass the Beanbag

Put all the beanbags in a basket or bucket. Invite children to find their own beanbag and pass the basket on. Use a stopwatch and challenge students to see how quickly they can empty the basket.

Extension: Ask all the children to close their eyes, reach in, and take a beanbag. When everyone has a beanbag, challenge students to give the beanbag they have to the person whose name is on it.

Beanbag Relay Race

Use just two beanbags for this. Start one beanbag around the circle one direction and the other beanbag around the circle the other direction. See which beanbag makes it back to you first. Invite different children to start the race. Do this several times and compare. "Does one direction always beat the other? Which direction? If this is the case, why do you think it's happening?"

Extensions: Have students pass the beanbags behind their backs or with their eyes closed.

Have each student put the beanbag on his head, then nod and tip it into the next student's lap.

Beanbag Circle Ending

Gather all the beanbags together. Instead of calling out names, hold up beanbags to dismiss the circle. The child whose beanbag is being held up claims it and puts it in her cubby.

Respect for the Classroom

Things go much more smoothly if everyone helps keep the classroom organized. Here are some activities for encouraging students to pitch in and help.

Pick It Up, Put It Back Game

Anytime the classroom is getting a little too chaotic, or it's time to move to a new activity or center, divide the class into two groups and challenge them to see which group can pick up an area fastest. Emphasize that the idea is to get things back where they belong *neatly*. Put some lively music on or sing the "Happy Helpers" song. At circle time, give stickers or some other award to both groups, one for winning and one for coming in a *very* close second.

Extensions: Challenge students to pair off and hold hands while picking up, or tie their legs together for a three-legged pick-up race.

Invite children to line up in two lines and do a relay pick-up.

The first child in line puts one thing away, then goes to the end of the line. This works best with older children.

"Happy Helpers" Song

(Sing to the tune of "Are You Sleeping?")

Happy helpers,

Happy helpers,

Pick up toys,

Pick up toys.

We make our classroom neat now,

We make our classroom neat now,

We're helping girls and boys.

We're helping girls and boys.

---

44   1-57029-526-3 *Social Development Activities for Circle Ti*
Getting Al

Neat Nick Flannel Board Story

Copy the next page on tagboard. Cut out the figures, color, and glue strips of felt on the back. Use to tell the following story:

Neat Nick

There once was a boy named Neat Nick. He had two brothers, named Grimy Gus and Messy Mel. They lived in a house in the forest and chopped wood for a living. Neat Nick always stacked his wood neatly, hung his hat up carefully, and was always tidy. Grimy Gus and Messy Mel would laugh at him and stack their wood any way. They never hung their hats up because they couldn't ever find them.

One day, the king was riding by. He saw Neat Nick's nice neat stack of wood.

"Young man," said the king, "that's the neatest stack of wood I've ever seen."

"Thank you, your majesty," said Neat Nick, politely doffing his hat. "My Granny always told me, 'a place for everything and everything in its place.'"

Grimy Gus and Messy Mel just stood there because, of course, they didn't have any hats to doff.

"You're such a fine young man. I want you to come to the palace and be my helper," the king said to Neat Nick. "The palace could use someone to organize it better. As for you two," the king said to Grimy Gus and Messy Mel, "it's the law that all men must doff their hats when the king passes by. Since you did not do so, I sentence you to three days in the dungeon."

So Neat Nick went to the castle and lived happily and well. As for Grimy Gus and Messy Mel, as soon as they got out of the dungeon, they went back to their hut to look for their hats, and are probably still looking for them.

Neat Nick Reproducible

Respect for the Earth

We all share the earth and need to show respect for our beautiful home.

Mother Earth Chant

(Sing to the tune of "London Bridge.")
This chant is based on a Native American song.

Mother Earth takes care of us,
Care of us,
Care of us.
Mother Earth takes care of us
Because she loves us so.

We take care of Mother Earth,
Mother Earth,
Mother Earth.
We take care of Mother Earth
Because we love her, too.

Earth Map Class Collage

Get a large map of the world and some travel magazines. Spread the map out in the center of the circle and invite students to look it over carefully. Point out the continents and the oceans. If you have a globe, compare the flat map and the globe. Point out where your town or city is. When the children have familiarized themselves with the map, encourage them to find pictures in the magazines of people, animals, ocean scenes, etc. Invite them to tear or cut out pictures and glue them to the map, with water pictures on the oceans and land pictures on the land masses. When the collage is complete, hang it up for everyone to admire. This is a very good use for out-of-date maps, which schools, libraries, and bookstores are usually happy to donate.

Extension: Make a Mother Earth Map Collage by asking children to find pictures of mothers and babies to use for the collage. This can be human mothers and babies or animal mothers and babies, or both.

 ## Nature Clean-Up Walk

This is a good activity to ask for parent volunteer help. At circle time, talk about how important it is that each of us does our part to keep nature clean. Divide into as many groups as you have grown-ups. Take some trash bags and rubber gloves and go around the block or to a nearby park and pick up any trash you find.

Extension: Invite children to make individual trash bags by decorating paper lunch sacks with potato stamps, etc. Use them for the trash walk, or have children take them home to use in their family cars.

 ## Adopt A . . .

As a class, decide on an environmental project you'd like to support. For example: "adopt" a whale or other endangered animal, save a piece of the rain forest, make a donation to the local animal shelter or a wildlife rescue facility. There are all sorts of good causes out there. Once you pick a project, spend some time during circle time deciding what you want to do to help. For instance, you could decorate oatmeal boxes and distribute them to local merchants to put out for donations, or bake cookies once a week and freeze the extras until you have enough for a bake sale to raise funds. As much as possible, let your students take the lead—which, believe me, they will.

 ## Thanks, Mom!

At circle time, invite children to think of things that Mother Nature provides for which they are grateful. Make a list and do a class mural, or encourage students to do individual pictures, of all the wonderful things they are thankful for.

The Three Earth Rs

Have a circle time discussion about the three "Rs" of conservation: Repair, Recycle, and Reuse. Ask, "Do you think it's important to use things more than once, if we can? Why? What are some ways that we could do this? Do you do any of these things at home?" and any other questions you can think of. Show your students the baskets listed below and model using them yourself as well as encouraging your students to do so.

Repair Basket

Have a basket for any toys that need repairing. Periodically have a "fix it" circle. Get out the repair basket and your tools, glue, etc. Invite students to help you fix what's been broken.

Recycle Basket

Have a basket for any articles, such as toilet paper tubes, that can be reused for art projects. Be sure to use recyclables regularly. Encourage children to bring recyclable items from home for classroom use. Have a list of items you use regularly, so parents can be aware of what to save.

Reuse Basket

Have a basket for students' outgrown clothes, shoes, coats, etc. Invite parents to check the basket for things their child might be able to use, and/or donate the items to a local homeless shelter. Keep some of the items on hand in case someone needs an emergency change of clothes. You could also collect toys to donate to a homeless shelter or children's hospital wing.

Learning to wait your turn is a vital part of the socialization process. Here are some enjoyable ways to help children learn what taking turns is all about.

Beanbag Chaos Game

Here is a good way to illustrate the reason for taking turns. Put all the beanbags into a pile in the center of the circle. On the count of three, everyone goes into the circle at once and tries to find his or her beanbag. This will probably turn into a bit of a free-for-all, but it's for a good cause. Once everyone has their beanbag and is sitting on the circle, put all the beanbags in a pile in the center again. This time, call on children, one at a time, to pick out their beanbag. Have a discussion afterwards including such questions as, "Was it easier for you to find your beanbag the first or second time? How did it feel when everyone was grabbing at the same time? Do you think it makes sense to take turns sometimes? Why?"

Extension: Get a stopwatch. Choose one student to time. See how long it takes her to find her beanbag during the free-for-all and how long it takes her to find it when everyone's taking turns.

"One at a Time" Song

(Sing to tune of "Are You Sleeping?")
Sing this any time children are waiting to take a turn.

One at a time
One at a time,
We take turns
We take turns,
That's the way
That's the way,
We all get to play.
We all get to play.

One Block at a Time

This is another good way to demonstrate the logic of taking turns. At circle time, have a bag or basket of building blocks. Show the blocks to your students and explain that you want to make a block tower. Ask, "What do you think will happen if I tip all the blocks out at the same time? Will doing that make a tower?" Tip the blocks out. "What happened? Did it make a tower?" Now position one block and put another one on top of it. "Will I be able to make a tower this way? Why?" Invite children to come, one at a time, and add a block to the tower. "Which do you think worked better, trying to do it all at once, or taking things one at a time?"

Extension: Attach a large sheet of paper to the wall. Have a rectangular sponge and a pie pan with red paint. Either draw the outline of a house on the paper or, for older students, simply explain that the class is going to make a picture of a house, one brick at a time. Invite students to take turns dipping the sponge into the paint and adding a "brick" to the picture. When it is done, invite them to make up a story about who lives in the house.

Story Chain

Hand out plastic links or large paper clips. Explain that you are going to take turns making a story chain. Start either a familiar story, such as "Goldilocks and The Three Bears" or simply make something up, such as "Once there was a boy named Tim who went for a walk. He went out the door and down the street. Suddenly he saw a . . ." Hand your link to the child next to you and instruct him to add his link to yours. Then, he tells the next part of the story and hands the chain to the next person, and so on. When you are finished, hold up the chain so the children can see how they all made it, link by link.

Extensions: Get a bag of small plastic animals and hand them out. Invite children to include the animal they got in their part of the story. Exchange animals and make up another story.

Transcribe the story—one page for each student's contribution—and invite them to illustrate it. Put it together for a class book and/or make copies for everyone to take home.

 # Mouse Turns Flannel Board Story

Copy the next page on tagboard. Cut out the figures, and color. Glue strips of felt on the back. Use to tell the following story:

Mouse Turns

Once there were four little mice who went out for a stroll. Suddenly, a cat began to chase them. The four little mice ran into an old boot. The boot was too small for the cat to fit into. It couldn't get to them, but they couldn't get out, either.

"Oh, dear," said the first little mouse, "If we stay in here, we will surely starve."

"On the other paw, if we try to leave, we will surely be eaten," said the second little mouse.

The third little mouse noticed some light coming in the toe of the boot.

"Look," he said, "there's a hole! We can sneak out that way."

All four mice ran to the hole. They pushed and shoved, all trying to get out of it at the same time, but the hole was too small.

Finally, the fourth little mouse said, "We're getting nowhere. This hole is only big enough for one of us at a time. Let's take turns."

So, the four little mice lined up and quietly, quietly, one at a time, they sneaked out of the boot—one, two, three, four—and ran straight home, leaving the hungry cat far behind.

Extensions: Invite students to take turns telling the story, using the flannel board pieces.

Invite students to act out the story.

Invite students to think of a different story with the same theme.

Mouse Turns Reproducible

Taking Turns Games

Teacher's Pet Game

It's nice to be the teacher's pet sometimes. Here's a great game that helps students learn to take turns and also gives them each a chance to be the center of attention. During circle time explain that you're going to play a guessing game and that each one of them is going to get to be the "teacher's pet" while the rest of the class tries to guess what kind of animal he or she is. Invite each student to come up to you. Whisper an animal name in their ear. They then act like that animal until someone guesses what they are. You might want to have a list prepared ahead of time, such as the following:

Bear	Cat	Dog	Snake	Elephant
Horse	Lion	Monkey	Bunny	Moose
Kangaroo	Mouse	Crocodile	Fish	Bee
Crab	Skunk	Rhino	Lizard	Bird

Whose Turn Is It?

Play this variation of "Who Stole the Cookie" to emphasize taking turns. Start by saying, "Whose turn is it to call on someone? It's (child's name) turn to call on someone." The child called on then says, "Who, me?" The rest of the class says, "Yes, you!" The child says, "Yes, I can." The rest say, "Who's next?" The child says, "It's (names another child's name) turn to call on someone." The second child then says, "Who, me?" and the game continues until everyone has had a turn.

Follow the Band Leader

For this game, children get to be band instruments. Go around the circle and invite each child to be the "band leader" and think of a sound to make, for instance, smacking lips or clapping hands or saying, "oompa, oompa." The rest of the class then makes the same sound. Encourage children to think of as many different sounds as possible. After everyone has had a turn being the "band leader," invite everyone to make the sound that they invented, all at the same time.

Extension: Challenge children to "play" a familiar song, such as "London Bridge" together, using the sounds they invented.

No, No, Your Turn

Play this variation of Duck, Duck, Goose to give students practice in turn-taking. Choose one child to be "it." Everyone is seated in the circle except for "it." It walks behind the other students, touching each one gently on the head while saying, "No, No, No," until she comes to the student she wants to tag and says, "Your turn!" That student then gets up and chases "it" around the circle. If it makes it back to where the chaser was sitting and manages to sit down without getting tagged, the chaser becomes "it." If the chaser touches "it" before she gets seated, that person stays "it" and has to try again. Make sure everyone has a turn before the game ends.

Rainbow Bridge

(Sing to the tune of "London Bridge")

Have two students face each other, one inside the circle and one outside, with their arms raised and their hands joined. Sing the following song as students take turns ducking under the upraised arms. Whoever is under the upraised arms at the end of the song takes the place of one of the "bridge" sides.

Rainbow Bridge is over you
Red and orange,
Yellow, too.
Green and purple,
Sky of blue
Hooray for colors!

Turn Around, Sit Down

This is a good transition from a standing to sitting circle activity. Teach the children the following chant. Then, when it's time to sit down, call names out one at a time. As each student follows the instructions, the rest can clap and chant along.

It's (child's name) turn
To turn around.
It's (child's name) turn
To sit right down.

ABCs of Taking Turns

Combine alphabet practice and taking turns with this activity. Get or make a set of cards with alphabet letters on them. Laminate them, punch a hole in one end, and tie a piece of string through the hole long enough to go over a child's head. Put all the cards in a bag and, when you are about to do an activity that involves taking turns, pass the bag around and invite each child to take one of the alphabet "necklaces" and put it on. The child who has the *A* takes the first turn, the child with the *B* takes the second turn, and so forth. If you have fewer than 26 children, just use as many letters as you have students. If you have more than 26, do both upper- and lowercase.

Extension: Make a sorting board by attaching 26 nails or cup hooks to a long board and mounting it on the wall where children can reach it. When you aren't using the ABC necklaces for turns, students can practice letter recognition by hanging them in the right order on the hooks. For very young children, put a letter sticker or decal above each hook so they can use it as a matching game.

Circus Circle

Explain to children that they are going to be in a circus act. First, go around the circle and invite children to choose an animal to pretend to be. Ask two students to hold a Hula Hoop™, sideways, above the ring. Play some lively music and encourage children to take turns going through the hoop the way their chosen animal would. For example: a bunny would hop through, a horse would gallop through, an elephant would lumber through, etc. They can keep going around the ring, doing the same animal or changing each time, whichever you and they prefer. Change hoop holders every so often so that everyone gets a turn.

Circle Crossing

This is a fun variation of "Simon Says." To play this game, everyone stands on the circle, facing in. Whoever is designated as "Simon" points at someone and gives directions for crossing the circle. For example: "Simon says skip across the circle." The child whose turn it is skips straight across the circle and stands on the line, facing out. "Simon" keeps going until all the children are facing outward.

Extension: For older children you can add the rule that, if "Simon" doesn't say "Simon Says," the child he points at can't move.

Small children like to share, provided they're not forced to do it all the time. Learning when and how to share is a skill we practice all our lives. Here are some ways to help your students get off to a good start in sharing.

Sharing Means Caring

We share because it's fair and to show that we care about others. Here are some ways to illustrate and practice these two very good reasons for sharing.

Take One and Pass It on Paper Chain

Have strips of colored paper, a marker, and a glue stick at the circle. Start a discussion about sharing by asking students what sorts of things they enjoy sharing with friends or family members. Pass the paper strips around, instructing each student to "take one and pass the rest on." When everyone has a strip, go around the circle and write what each child said he enjoyed sharing on his strip. Pass the glue stick around and (with a bit of help, if necessary) make a paper chain out of the strips. Hang it on the wall, or drape it on a plant.

Sharing Fair

Plan a sharing fair. Do some or all of the following:

✦ Request that students each bring in one part of a snack to share. For example, a third of the class could bring in crackers, a third could bring in cheese, and a third could bring in apple juice. At snack time, have everyone help assemble the snack and share it.

✦ Encourage children to bring a special toy (but not so special that they can't bear to share it). At circle time, have a show-and-tell of their toys. During free play, encourage a lot of toy sharing.

✦ Collect cans of food or clothing to share with a local soup kitchen or homeless shelter.

✦ Invite grandparents or other elders in to share their memories and stories with the children.

 # Fair Share of the Pizza Dry-Erase Board Story

Tell this story while illustrating it on a dry-erase board.

Fair Share of the Pizza

Tony baked himself a pizza. *(Draw a circle on the board.)*

Sheila came into the kitchen. "Yum, yum, " she said. "That pizza smells good!"

"I will share my pizza with you," said Tony. He cut the pizza into two pieces. *(Draw a vertical line down the center of the circle, making two equal halves.)*

Daddy and Mommy came home from work. "Yum, yum," they said. "That pizza smells good!"

"I will share my pizza with you, too," said Tony. He cut the pizza into four pieces. *(Draw a horizontal line across the center of the pizza, making four equal quarters.)*

Grandma and Grandpa came in. "Yum, yum," they said. "That pizza smells good!"

"I will share my pizza with you, too," said Tony. He cut the pizza into six pieces. *(Draw a diagonal line across the circle, through two of the four quarters.)*

"Hey," said Sheila, "That's not fair. Some people will get big pieces and some will get little ones." "You're right," said Tony. "It's not fair. What should I do?" Just then, George the dog and Sam the cat came into the kitchen. They didn't say anything, but they sniffed very loudly.

"I know," said Tony. "I will share my pizza with George and Sam, too." *(Draw another diagonal line across the circle, making eight equal pieces.)* "There," said Tony. "Now everyone will get a fair share!"

"Hooray," said Sheila and Daddy and Mommy and Grandpa and Grandma. George said, "Woof!" and Sam said, "Meow!" Then everyone ate their fair share of the pizza. "Yum, yum!"

Extensions: Have the children help you count the pieces each time the pizza is cut.

Make copies of the pizza reproducible on the next page. Use them for art or math practice or both.

Have pizza for lunch. Make sure everyone gets a fair share!

Fair Share of the Pizza Reproducible

Color the pizza below and cut it into fair shares for your family.

"Share, Share, Share with Friends" Song

(Sing to the tune of "Row, Row, Row Your Boat.")

Share, share, share with friends

That is what we do.

If you will share your

Things with me,

I'll share my things

With you.

Sharing Stars

Use the pattern below to cut a star shape out of yellow poster board. Write *I'm a Sharing Star* on it with silver ink or glitter. Glue a safety pin to the back or punch a hole in the top point and string it on a piece of yarn. When you see a student being a good sharer, acknowledge her at circle time and let her wear the "sharing star" for the rest of the day.

Share the Air

Start a circle discussion about the many things that we share as a matter of course by saying, "Every day we all share the air we breath. What else do we all share?" See how many things your students can come up with that everyone shares. Remind them to think in terms of all five of their senses. "What sights do we all share? What sounds do we all share? What things can we all smell, touch, taste?"

Share the Wealth

Get some chocolate coins, two for each student. See if any of your students have heard the word *talent*. If so, let them tell you what it is. If not, explain that, nowadays, a talent is anything someone can do especially well. However, long ago there was also a type of money called a "talent." Discuss the fact that no one has exactly the same abilities, but everyone has their own talents—their own "wealth"—to share. Ask students to think of something they can do very well. This can be anything from being able to throw a ball to giving really good hugs. Prompt any student that needs a little help thinking of something. Once everyone has thought of a talent, go around the circle again and see if they can think of a way to share their talent with someone else. Give each child two coins, to represent their talent. Invite them to choose someone in the circle that they would like to share their talent with, and give one of their "talent" coins to that person. Make sure everyone ends up with two coins—one of their own and one of someone else's—because no one loses their talent by sharing it.

Extension: If your classroom is sugar-free, or you have students who have chocolate allergies, use plastic coins.

Sharing Is Special

There are many categories of "special needs" these days. Chances are you have one or more students in your class who have been given some sort of a "special needs" label. The truth is, however, that everyone has special needs, it's just that some are more obvious than others. Help children see this by having a talking bear sharing session about what each student thinks his or her special needs are. Point out that there are some needs that everybody shares, such as needing love and respect, regardless of what individual special needs they have.

Sharing Is Fun!

Sharing Scales

Get some shiny wrapping paper, the holographic type would be ideal. Cut it into 4-inch squares, one for each of your students. Read the book *Rainbow Fish* by Marcus Pfister and J. Alison James (Nord-Sud Verlag, 1992) during circle time. Ask, "Why did Rainbow Fish decide to share his scales? Do you think he was happier before or after he shared? Have you shared something that was hard to share? How did you feel?"

Hand out the wrapping paper squares and go around the circle, asking each student to name something special that they have and would be willing to share. Write their answers on the "scales." Make a large fish shape out of butcher paper and attach it to the wall or bulletin board. Invite students to tape their "sharing scales" onto the fish.

Extension: Have a day when everyone brings the special thing they listed to class. Take the scales off the fish and put them in a bag. Invite each child to pull a scale out of the bag. When everyone has a scale, they give the person who picked their scale the item they brought to share. After everyone has had some time with the shared items, give them back to their owners and put the scales back on the fish.

Intangibles Sharing Circle

It's not just *things* that people share. Using your talking bear, go around the circle and invite children to share stories, songs, memories, jokes, or other "intangibles" that they feel like sharing. Point out that this kind of sharing is especially nice because what you share you also get to keep, so everybody ends up with more than they started with.

Share That Hug

Occasionally end your circle by having everybody get into the center and share a big old bear hug. It feels great!

Trail Mix Sharing

Multi-task by combining a nice day, counting practice, and a sharing exercise. Instead of an indoor snack and circle time, go outside and sit in a circle on a blanket or in the grass. Give children small cups or plastic bags to hold their snacks. Have several bags of "trail mix" type snack items, such as peanuts, dried fruit, cheese cubes, etc., for sharing. Designate several "official sharers," one for each item. (Pre-count so you will how many of each item is available per student. For instance, four peanuts and two cheese cubes.) Ask the "official sharers" to count out the proper number of items as they share. Encourage the other children to count along. After snack, share a favorite circle game.

Sharing Rhyme

To illustrate why sharing is fun, get two similar toys, such as trucks or dinosaurs, and act out sharing them while saying this poem. Invite students to take turns being the "sharer" and the "sharee."

When I have two toys and you have none
We cannot play, which isn't fun.
So here is what I'm going to do,
I'm going to share my toys with you.
Here's one for you. Now we each have one.
Let's play together. Oh, what fun!

Feel Good Sharing Circle

One of the intangibles that it's important to share is our feelings. Not so much our bad feelings, as those get aired pretty regularly, but the nice feelings we have and forget to mention. Every so often, have a "feel good sharing circle" and invite students to share a nice feeling they've had about someone else in the class. You might start it out by going around the circle and saying something nice about each student such as "I was so happy when Sally remembered to use her table manners at snack time. It made me feel good when John thanked me for tying his shoe, etc."

Strawberry Share

Read the story, *The Little Mouse, the Red Ripe Strawberry and the Big Hungry Bear* by Audrey and Don Wood (Child's Play International, Ltd., 1984) aloud at circle time. Ask some questions, such as "Why did the mouse decide to share the strawberry? Have you ever had so much of something that you decided to share it just so it wouldn't go to waste? What? Who did you share it with?"

Extensions: Cut a strawberry out of red construction paper and invite students to act out the story.

Read this book during strawberry season and pass around a bowl of strawberries to share afterwards.

Share and Share Alike

Start a discussion about sharing by mentioning the old saying "Share and share alike." Explain that it means when people share something everyone should each get an equal, or like, amount. Illustrate this concept by having six blocks, cars, or other items. Ask three children to come and sit in front of you. Give one item to the first child, two to the second, and three to the third. Ask if everyone thinks all three children got a fair share of the items. See if the three children can sort out how to make things even. With older children, consider using more children and items.

Extension: Divide into groups of three and give each group nine items. See if they can figure out how to "share and share alike."

"Thanks for Sharing" Song

When a student brings a snack or something else to share, sing this song to the tune of "So Long, It's Been Good to Know You."

Thank you, for caring and sharing,

Thank you, for caring and sharing,

Thank you, for caring and sharing,

That was a nice thing to do.

As children grow, they learn how to be more and more responsible, that is more and more "able to respond" to the world around them. We help them do this by modeling and encouraging responsible behaviors and by being understanding about mistakes, both theirs and ours.

Chores and Privileges

There are some things we have to do, such as brushing our teeth, and some things we get to do, such as going to a party. Here are some ideas for encouraging students to take their chores in stride, and appreciate their privileges.

Classroom Chore Sticks

Write students' names on craft sticks, one name per stick. Invite students to decorate them with stickers, glitter, etc. Keep the sticks in the "Chore Stick" cup as described on page 12. At the beginning of circle time, take as many sticks out of the cup as there are chores to do. Distribute them, one to a "chore" cup. When a child finishes her chore, she takes her stick out of the "chore" cup and puts it into the "Done" cup. Keep doing this each day until all the "chore sticks" are in the "Done" cup. Put them all back into the "Chore Stick" cup and start over.

Extension: Instead of chore cups, get a shoe bag and put a different chore for each pocket.

When all the chore sticks have made it to the "Done" cup, put on some music and dance around the circle to celebrate, or sing the following song:

"Chore" Song

(Sing to the tune of "Heigh Ho.")
Sing this song once all the chore sticks are in the "Done" cup.

Hooray!
Hooray!
We did our chores today.
We lend a hand
Because we can.
And now
It's time for us to play.
Hooray!

Helping Hands Tree

Using a sheet of butcher paper, make a large outline of a Christmas tree shape on the bulletin board. Keep some green construction paper handy. When you see a student being particularly helpful, draw an outline of his hand on the green paper and invite him to cut it out. Write his name and what he did on the handprint and glue it to the outline, starting at the bottom and working up. When the tree is full, invite children to decorate the tree with glitter, stickers, etc.

Extensions: Instead of a tree, mount the handprints on a sheet of paper and send home to parents.

When the tree is finished, invite parents and have a special "helping hands" party to celebrate.

I'm a Home Helper

At circle time, ask each student to complete the sentence. *I'm a home helper when I _____.* After each child says what she does to help at home, invite her to stand up and take a bow, while the other students clap.

At art time, suggest that students draw pictures of themselves helping at home.

It's a Privilege

Here's a circle time activity to help students begin to sort out the difference between privileges and responsibilities. Start a discussion by pointing out that every privilege has a responsibility attached. For example: It's a privilege to have a pet, and a responsibility to feed it. See if your students can come up with more examples. During art time, invite them to draw a picture of a privilege on one side of a piece of paper and a matching responsibility on the other.

"I'm Responsible" Song

(Sing to the tune of "The Farmer in the Dell.")

Oh, I'm responsible.

Oh, I'm responsible.

When I feed my cat

Or hang up my hat

I'm being responsible.

When I'm responsible,

When I'm responsible,

My mom and dad

And teacher are glad,

When I'm responsible.

P and R Coin

Cut a large letter *P* out of textured fabric and glue it onto a round piece of cardboard that is covered with foil. Cut an *R* out of a different fabric and glue it onto the other side of the cardboard. Start a circle discussion by showing students the circle and telling them that this is a "privilege and responsibility coin," because privileges and responsibilities are two sides of the same coin. Trace the *P* with your finger and say, "*P* is for privilege. It is a privilege to be your teacher." Turn the coin over and trace the *R* and say, "*R* is for responsibility. My responsibility as your teacher is to teach you good things." Invite children to take turns holding the coin and talking about their privileges and responsibilities.

Oops!

Children need to learn that making mistakes is okay. It's easier to take responsibility for our gaffs if they're seen as an expected and accepted part of life.

Spilled Milk

At circle time, tell your students the old saying, "There's no use crying over spilled milk." Ask if they know what this means. If you like, you might read the Aesop fable about the milkmaid who was daydreaming and spilled the milk she was carrying. Discuss the fact that everybody makes mistakes and that's okay. Then, teach them the following song.

"Everybody Makes Mistakes" Song

(Sing to the tune of "London Bridge.")

Everybody makes mistakes, makes mistakes, makes mistakes.
Everybody makes mistakes,
And that's okay.

Spilled milk isn't worth your tears, worth your tears, worth your tears.
Spilled milk isn't worth your tears,
Don't let it spoil your day.

Pick It Up, Wipe It Up Chant

Do this chant with accompanying movements during circle time, then remind students of it when there's a spill to deal with.

Pick it up,	*Lean over and mime picking something up.*
Wipe it up,	*Make circular wiping motions with hands.*
Put it in the trash.	*Mime throwing something away.*
That's what we do	*Dust hands together.*
When anything goes CRASH!	*Throw hands in air on CRASH.*
Pick it up,	*Lean over and mime picking something up.*
Wipe it up,	*Make circular wiping motions with hands.*
Put it in the trash.	*Mime throwing something away.*
That's what we do	*Dust hands together.*
When anything goes SPLASH!	*Throw arms wide on SPLASH.*

Sir Fix It Story

To tell this story, you need an apron with pockets, or a basket. Have the following items in the basket or apron pockets: a roll of clear tape, a stapler, a bottle of glue, and some string. Take the items out as you come to them in the story.

Sir Fix It

In the land of Oopsalot, there was a royal family named King Spill, Queen Drop, and their two children, Princess Whoopsie Daisy and Prince Fumble. Unfortunately, the whole royal family was very clumsy, so clumsy that practically everything in the castle was broken.

"Oh, woe is me," said King Spill one day. "My favorite book is torn and I can no longer read it."

"Well, all my best recipes keep coming out of their cover and falling on the floor," said Queen Drop. "Cook has refused to use them anymore."

"You think that's bad? All my chess pieces are broken," said Princess Whoopsie Daisy.

"Well, I can't fly my kite at all," said Prince Fumble. "There's not a piece of string more than two inches long in the whole castle."

A knight in shining armor strode into the room. "Sire," he said. "My name is Sir Fix It. I have heard of your plight and am prepared to mend and repair."

"Wonderful! If you can fix my book, the queen's recipes, the princess' chess pieces, and the prince's kite, I will give you half my kingdom!" said King Spill.

Sir Fix It got right to work. First he took out some—what? *(Hold up tape.)* That's right, tape to mend the king's book. Then he took out—what? *(Hold up stapler.)* Yes, his stapler and stapled all the queen's recipes back into their folder. Then he pulled out some—what? *(Hold up glue bottle.)* That's right, glue and fixed all the princess' chess pieces, paying special attention to the knights, of course. Last, he reached into his pocket and found some—what? *(Hold up string.)* Right again, string for the prince's kite.

King Spill was delighted. He gave Sir Fix It half his kingdom then and there. Sir Fix It renamed his half of the kingdom Canfixalot. He paid regular visits to Oopsalot with his—what? *(Hold up tape, stapler, glue and string.)* And they all lived happily ever after.

69

I Can Do It!

Nothing builds self-esteem like being able to do things for oneself. Here are some great "can do" activities.

"Can Do" Song

(Sing to the tune of "Are You Sleeping?")
Whenever a student masters a new skill, celebrate by singing this song at circle time.

(child's name) can do it.
(child's name) can do it.
Yes, s/he can,
Yes, s/he can.
(child's name) can (skill) now,
(child's name) can (skill) now.
So we say
Hip, hip, hooray!

Cancan Dance

Stand on the line and show everyone how to dance like a cancan dancer: Tap the floor with your right foot, then raise the right knee, tap the floor with your right foot again, then kick your right leg straight out and up. Reverse. Trust me, anyone can do this with a little practice, including you.

"Yes I Cancan" Song

(Sing this while you are dancing, to the tune of the "Yes I Cancan" song.)

Oh, I can-can do so many,
I can do so many,
Things and so can you,
And so can you.

Let's all sing and do the can-can.
Just because I can-can.
Yes, and so can you,
And so can you.

Bunny Bow Story

Tying a bow is an important skill to learn, but getting a chance to practice it is harder since the advent of Velcro™ shoe fastenings. Here's an engaging story to help children learn the basics of bow tying. Use the bunny reproducible on the next page to make a tagboard bunny for each student. Thread a shoelace through the two "ear holes." Make sure the ends are even, and tape securely in the back. Get out the bunnies every so often at circle time so everyone can practice "bunny bows" together.

Bunny Bow Story

Once there was a bunny with very l-o-o-n-g ears.

Hold up the shoelace ends.

One day, he was running here and there through the forest.

Take one shoelace and weave it over and under the other one.

Suddenly, he heard a dog barking, "Woof, woof!"

"Oh, dear," said the bunny. "I must go back to my burrow! But where is it?"

He looked around and saw a familiar bush.

Form a loop with one shoelace.

He ran around the bush and saw a hole.

Take the other shoelace and loop it around the first one.

"Thank goodness, there's my burrow," he said, and ran inside.

Complete tying the bow.

The bunny was glad to be safe, but surprised to see that his ears were much shorter.

Hold up the loops so everyone can see the bunny's bow tied "ears."

Bunny Bow Reproducible

72 1-57029-526-3 *Social Development Activities for Circle Ti*
Getting Al

So much of life takes teamwork and cooperation. Here are some activities to encourage your students to make cooperating a way of life, in and out of the classroom.

Coop-eration

Chicken Run Activities

Have a special movie day and watch *Chicken Run*. Later, in circle time, talk about the movie and discuss the fact that it took all the chickens working together to escape from the Tweedy's farm. Do some or all of the following activities to emphasize the idea of "coop-eration."

✦ Ask, "If you had an airplane that could take you anywhere, where would you go?" Discuss various ideas until you agree on a destination. Take a pretend flight to your chosen destination by inviting students to lie on their backs, with their feet in the air and peddle, like the chickens did in the movie. Encourage them to do some pretending, such as, "We're high above the clouds now, time to circle the landing field, we're coming in for a landing, etc."

✦ Ask students to kneel on the circle, heads down and hands tucked in their armpits. Use a medium-sized ball or a large plastic egg. If using a ball, explain that it is an "egg" and everyone needs to cooperate to get it all the way around the inside of the circle, using their "beaks" and "wings."

✦ Using the students' circle spots, make a "pie obstacle course" across the circle by scattering the spots in the middle of the circle. Take turns running across the circle. Invite children to decide if they want to be "Rocky" who stepped in all the pies, or "Ginger" who stepped around them.

✦ At the end of the movie, the chickens told their chicks the story of their great escape. Invite students to tell an adventure, real or imagined, that they have had. Use a plastic talking egg for this instead of the usual talking bear.

Coop-eration Flannel Board Story

Copy page 75 on tagboard. Cut out the figures, color, and glue strips of felt on the back. Use to tell the following story:

Coop-eration

Once upon a time, all chickens were wild. So were all ducks and geese and turkeys. The chickens slept out in the open, on tree branches, and they got hardly any sleep, what with watching for tigers and foxes and wolves who might want to eat them. The ducks and geese stayed out in the middle of the lake to be safe, and didn't get much sleep, either. The turkeys slept crouched in the longest grass they could find, and they were the most nervous of all.

One day, a chicken named Charlotte called a meeting of her friends, Darla Duck, Geraldine Goose, and Trina Turkey.

"I'm a nervous wreck and I don't dare lay any eggs," she said. "I'm so tired of sleeping in trees. I want to live somewhere safe."

"Me, too," said Darla. "My feet are all wrinkled from being in the water so much."

"So are mine," said Geraldine. "What I wouldn't give for a nice, warm *dry* place to sleep."

"Well, I *have* a nice warm, dry place," said Trina. "And let me tell you, it's not all it's cracked up to be. I'm a nervous wreck!"

"Maybe, if we all work together, we can make ourselves a house that's safe and warm and dry, with room for each of us to have a nest and raise a family," suggested Charlotte.

"I'll give anything a try," said Darla. Geraldine and Trina said it sounded like a good idea to them.

For days and days the four friends worked, hauling tree branches and logs, and tying them together with vines. At last they were done. They had built a fine, sturdy little house with room for all of them and a strong door to keep the tigers and foxes and wolves away from them and their eggs.

"This is wonderful," sighed Geraldine, as they all settled down for their first night of sound, safe sleep.

"What shall we call our new home?" asked Trina. "It ought to have a name."

"Let's call it our 'coop,'" suggested Charlotte, "because we all had to coop-erate to build it."

So, to this day, houses for chickens and ducks and geese and turkeys are still called coops.

Coop-eration Reproducible

Spring into Cooperation Party

Celebrate spring and cooperation at the same time with a party featuring some or all of the following ideas:

Chocolate Egg Relay Race

At circle time, equip everyone with a plastic spoon. The object of this race is to pass a chocolate egg all the way around the circle, from spoon to spoon, without using any hands.

Cooperation Egg Hunt

Hide plastic, hard-boiled, or chocolate eggs around the classroom, one per student. Once a student has found an egg, he stops hunting and sits in the middle of the circle. If someone is having a hard time finding her egg, she can ask the children sitting in the circle to help her look. If you hide them well, it will take a lot of cooperation for all the eggs to be found.

Pass the Egg Guessing Game

Get an egg-shaped bead and string it onto a piece of string or yarn long enough to go around the circle. One child is "it." "It" sits in the middle of the circle with her eyes closed. The other children all hold onto the string and slide the "egg" from hand to hand until "it" says stop and opens her eyes. Everyone keeps their hands on the string, and "it" guesses which person is holding the "egg." If she guesses correctly, that person becomes "it."

"Egg"-ceptionally Good Egg Salad

Boil half as many eggs as you have students. Ask children to help you peel them. This is a good activity for an outdoor circle. If the eggs are colored, save the shells, crunch them into bits and make mosaic pictures with them. Chop the whites and yolks up fine and add enough mayonnaise to moisten well, usually about a teaspoon per egg. Add 1/8 teaspoon mustard and 1/4 teaspoon dill weed for every two eggs. Stir well and serve on crackers or bread.

All Together Now

Cooperating means "doing things together." Try some of these great group activities.

Class Amoeba

Explain that amoebas are tiny, one-celled animals. If possible, find a picture of an amoeba to show your students. Tell them that you are going to become a "class amoeba." Ask everyone to join hands. You are now a single creature and have to cooperate in order to survive. If anyone loses their grip, your amoeba will die. Lead the amoeba around the classroom, or go outside and walk around the playground.

Extensions: Try to perform a task without letting go of hands, such as picking up a basketball or moving a chair.

If you are outside and there are any trees around, see if your amoeba can get completely around the tree. (Hint: To do this, some children will need to put their backs to the tree.)

With older children, try passing something small from hand to hand, all the way around the amoeba.

Story Web

Weave a story together. At circle time, have a large ball of yarn handy. Begin a familiar story or use a story starter such as "Once upon a time there was a princess with a terrible problem." Hang onto the end of the yarn and throw the ball to someone across the circle. They add more to the story, then hold onto the yarn where they caught it and throw the ball to someone else. Continue until everyone has had a turn adding to the story and admire the beautiful "story web" you just wove.

Nature Web

Talk about the way everything in nature cooperates and is connected. Weave a nature web much like you did the story web. Think of a plant or animal and another plant or animal it cooperates with or is connected to. For example, you might say, "Owls eat mice." Throw the yarn ball to someone else, who says how the web continues, such as "Mice eat corn or mice are food for cats," and so on.

77

1-57029-526-3 *Social Development Activities for Circle Time: Getting Along*

Ready, Set, Relay

Relays races are great practice in cooperation. Circle relays are nice to do because there's no need to divide up into teams. Use a stopwatch and encourage students to set a new record each time around the circle. That way, everybody gets to be a winner.

 ## Baby Relay

For this relay you need a baby bonnet, a bib, and a rattle. As fast as he can, the first person puts on the bonnet and bib, shakes the rattle, then takes everything off and hands it to the next person, who does the same, and so on around the circle. For younger children use a bonnet and bib with Velcro™ fastenings. For older children, bows or buttons are a good challenge.

 ## Feather Relay

Hand out straws and ask everyone to get down on their hands and knees. Put a feather in front on one of your students and explain that the object of this relay is to get the feather all the way around the circle by blowing on it through the straws. This is fairly easy if you have a tile floor and more of a challenge on carpet.

 ## Water Relay

Do this one outside on a hot day. Provide everyone with a paper cup and see if they can pour water from cup to cup all the way around the circle, without spilling any.

 ## Pumpkin Relay

Provide everyone with a small paper plate and see if they can pass a mini pumpkin all the way around the circle, from plate to plate, without using their hands or dropping the pumpkin.

Parachute Fun

Use a parachute, blanket, or round tablecloth for these great cooperative activities.

Ring Around the Parachute

Everyone holds onto the edge of the parachute and walks in a circle, saying the following chant and doing matching actions:

Ring around the parachute,
Ring around the parachute,
Down and up
And we all run under.

Cooperative Ball Rolling

Put a large ball in the middle of the parachute. See if everyone can work together to get the ball to roll to a specific person.

Extension: For older children, put as many small, light balls, such as Ping-Pong™ balls, as you have students, in the middle of the parachute. Give the parachute a good fling, then drop it and see how many children can catch one of the balls.

Siamese Turtle

This is a variation on the amoeba activity. Tell children that they are going to be "Siamese turtles," all sharing the same shell. Invite them to stand, facing outward and hold their part of the parachute around their neck, like a cape. See if everyone can work together to walk around the room or yard without letting go of their "shell."

Parachute Cradle

Invite one child to lie in the middle of the blanket. The others work together to lift him up a few inches and rock him *gently* while singing a lullaby. Encourage children to take turns. This is a good trust-building exercise.

Extension: If you don't have a sturdy enough parachute or blanket for this, or you feel your class is a bit too rowdy to be gentle enough with each other's bodies, use a stuffed animal.

Community Cooperation

It takes a lot of cooperation for a community to function. Children like to feel like they are a contributing part of that effort. Spend some circle time choosing a class community project, either from the list below or whatever is needed in your particular community, and work on it together.

✦ Adopt a section of a local roadway and spend a Saturday morning every few months with your students and their families doing a cooperative clean-up.

✦ Contact a retirement home or assisted living center and see if any of their guests would like to become honorary grandparents for your class. Invite them to visit and read or tell stories at circle time. Encourage students to work together to make holiday cards and gifts for individuals and/or the center.

✦ Instead of a road, adopt a local park or playground. Spend some time every few weeks cleaning it up. See if you can get permission to plant some flowers in the spring, or hang bird feeders in the winter.

✦ Bake cupcakes together once a month to give to a local group that helps keep the community running, such as the ambulance association, rotary club, town hall employees, etc. Ask someone from the group to come collect the cupcakes and talk to your students about their work.

✦ Work with the local Humane Society to organize a Pet Adoption Day and see how many new homes you can find for abandoned animals.

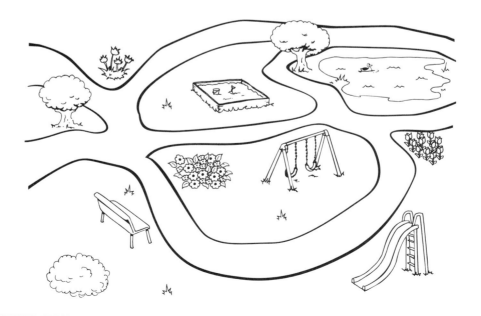

Books About Getting Along

The books listed below are helpful to encourage getting along and being polite.

Oops! Excuse Me Please: And Other Mannerly Tales by Bob McGrath and Tammie Lyon (Barron's Educational Series, 1998)

Monster Manners by Bethany Roberts (Clarion Books, 1996)

Taking Turns by Janine Amos and Annabel Spenceley (Gareth Steven Publishing, 2002)

We Can Get Along: A Child's Book of Choices by Lauren Murphy Payne and Claudia Rohling (Free Spirit Publishing, 1997)

Chrysanthemum by Kevin Henkes (HarperTrophy, 1996)

Just Because I Am: A Child's Book of Affirmations by Lauren Murphy Payne and Claudia Rohling (Free Spirit Publishing, 1994)

Will I Have a Friend? by Miriam Cohen (Aladdin; Reprint edition 1989)

Share and Take Turns and the rest of the *Learning to Get Along Series* by Cheri J. Meiners and Meredith Johnson (Free Spirit Publishing, 2003)

Timothy Goes to School by Rosemary Wells (Puffin Books, Reissue Edition 2000)

I Like Being Me: Poems for Children, About Feeling Special, Appreciating Others, Getting Along by Judy Lalli and Douglas L. Mason-Fry (Free Spirit Publishing 1997)

A Porcupine Named Fluffy by Helen Lester (Houghton Mifflin/Walter Lorraine Books, 1989)

Peace isn't just something that happens when nobody's fighting. It is created moment by moment both in the classroom and the world. Help your students learn that peace is a choice we always have available to us.

Apologies Accepted

Everybody says and does things that they wish they hadn't. In order to get along, it is important to know when and how to apologize.

"I'm Sorry" Poem

During circle time, teach children this poem to use whenever they are having a hard time apologizing.

It's hard for me to admit
That I've done something wrong.

I wish what I did would just go away
So we could get along.

I know that I have hurt you, though,
And the hurt won't go away.

Until I apologize. So I'm ready
To shake your hand and say

I'm sorry.

Circle Sorry

Have a circle discussion about apologizing. "Why do people say they're sorry? Have you been sorry about something you did? How did you feel? Did you say you were sorry? How did that feel?" If there are any apologies that need to be made in the class, this would be a good time and place to clear the air.

 # Peace Rose

Once your students grasp this process, they will begin putting it into practice with amazing results. Get a silk or plastic rose. Show it to the children at circle time and explain that this is the class peace rose. Invite two students to stand in the middle of the circle and help you demonstrate how the rose works. The steps are as follows:

✦ When two children have a fight or disagreement, they go get the peace rose.

✦ Using it like the talking bear, they take turns holding it and discussing the problem, looking each other in the eye and using "I feel" messages, such as "I didn't like it when you grabbed the truck" or "I was angry because I asked for a turn but you ignored me."

✦ Acknowledge that they heard each other, and apologize if appropriate. "I can see why you were mad that I didn't give you a turn. Sorry. I guess I'd be mad, too, if someone grabbed something out of my hands. Sorry."

✦ State what each is willing to do to correct the problem. "I did have the truck for a long time; you can play with it now. Let's each count to 20 when the other one has the truck, so we each get a fair turn."

✦ When both children are satisfied, they hold the rose together and say, "Peace is possible!"

Remind children to use the peace rose when disagreements arise. Encourage them to practice the three *I* communication skills: (eye contact, I feel messages, what I will do).

 # Peace Bubbles

Native Americans used to share a peace pipe when they met, as a symbol of goodwill. The next time you have an outside circle, pass around a bottle of bubbles and a bubble wand. Encourage everyone to blow some bubbles as a symbol of goodwill.

Heart of Peace Dry-Erase Board Story

Tell this story while illustrating it on a dry-erase board:

Heart of Peace

Once there were two very good friends named Sally and Joe. *(Make two dots close together near the bottom of the board.)* One day they had a big fight. Sally was sure that she was right. Joe was just as sure that he was. Neither one would listen to the other.

"I'm never going to speak to you again!" said Sally. "I'm going home!" *(Draw a line from the left dot, angled left and up.)*

"Well," said Joe. "If that's the way you want to be, I'm never going to speak to you again, either!" *(Draw a line up from the right dot angled right and up.)*

After a few days, Sally began to feel very lonely.

"I miss Joe. I'm going to go see him and apologize," said Sally. "After all, our fight was as much my fault as his." *(Curve the left line up, around and toward the center, making half a heart shape.)*

Joe missed Sally, too.

"I want to make up with Sally," said Joe. "I'm really sorry I said the things I did. I hope she'll talk to me." *(Curve the left line up, around and toward the center, making the other half of the heart shape.)*

"I'm sorry, Joe," said Sally as soon as she saw him.

"I'm sorry, too, Sally," said Joe. "From now on, let's meet each other halfway, instead of fighting, okay?"

"Okay," Sally agreed.

Joe and Sally were friends from then on. They had learned how to find the "heart of peace" by saying they were sorry.

 # Peace Heart Valentines

Invite each child to think of something he could do to make the classroom more peaceful. Pass some red paper and scissors around the circle and encourage children to cut out a heart shape (pre-cut hearts for younger children). Write their peaceful idea on their heart. At art time, decorate the hearts with glitter, stickers, etc. Exhibit the hearts around the classroom for Valentine's Day.

 # Sincere Apologies

Have a discussion about the fact that *saying* sorry isn't necessarily the same as *feeling* sorry. Suggest that, instead of just saying sorry, students also say what they will do to *show* that they are sorry. Encourage children to think of times, from their own experience, when actions would have been better than words. Invite them to act out their stories, if they like.

 # I Just Called to Say "I'm Sorry"

Sometimes it's hard to apologize face to face. Try this exercise in circle time to use in class when needed. Get two toy phones. Ask two students to sit back to back, each with a telephone. Ask one student to imagine some reason why they need to apologize to the other student. Prompt him a bit if he can't think of something. Invite him to "call" the other student and apologize. Coach the other student to accept the apology graciously. Switch roles. After everyone gets the idea, any time someone is having a hard time making an apology to another student, ask if he'd rather make a "sorry call."

Peaceful Classroom

Help create a peaceful classroom with these circle time activities.

Lizards Inside, Dinosaurs Outside

To illustrate the difference between "indoor" and "outdoor" voices, do this activity. Ask everyone to stand up just outside the circle line. Explain that this is dinosaur land. This is like being outdoors where it's okay to roar as loud as a dinosaur. Encourage everyone to roar and stomp around a bit. Now, invite students to step inside the circle. This is lizard land. As everyone knows, lizards are very quiet. Encourage everyone to tiptoe and talk softly. Invite students to step back and forth across the circle and practice their dinosaur and lizard voices. Remind them to be lizards inside and keep their dinosaur voices for outside.

Stomp, Stomp, Stomp; Tippy, Tippy, Toe Chant

Practice indoor, outdoor noise levels with this chant. March around the circle as you chant it.

Stomp, Stomp, Stomp,
Tippy, Tippy, Toe,
'Round and 'round the circle we go.

Outdoors we make
LOTS OF NOISE.
Indoors we're
Quiet girls and boys.

Quiet Music Circle Dancing

When things are getting too noisy, put on some quiet music and invite children to dance around the circle as quietly as snowflakes or feathers or autumn leaves or . . . what's the quietest thing they can think of?

Extension: Have some chiffon or silk scarves for students to wave as they dance.

Peaceful Classroom, Crazy Classroom

Have a discussion about what makes a peaceful classroom, and what makes a crazy classroom. For example, ask, "Which makes the classroom more peaceful, loud voices or quiet voices? etc." Work as a group to make a chart of peaceful behaviors and crazy making behaviors. Draw a line across the middle of the chart and write the peaceful behaviors above the line and the crazy-making behaviors below the line. Point out when someone's behavior is below the line. Be sure to also regularly recognize and commend above the line behaviors.

Peace Lights

Get Christmas lights and fasten them up in a conspicuous place in the classroom. For example, run them around the top of the wall, or string them on a large plant. At circle time, explain that these are peace lights, to remind students that this is a peaceful classroom. When things are getting too rowdy, you will turn the main light off so that only the peace lights are on, as a gentle, non-verbal reminder for people to calm down. Practice this several times to make sure students grasp the concept.

Extension: Instead of Christmas lights, get a flashlight. Turn the overhead lights off for a moment and flash the flashlight to get students' attention.

Peace Pilgrim Walk

At circle time, tell students the story of "Peace Pilgrim," a woman who spent 28 years walking more than 25,000 miles, back and forth across America, to inspire people to be more peaceful. Make a U.S.-shaped outline on the floor in the center of the circle with tape or chalk. Invite students to pretend that they are Peace Pilgrims and encourage them to walk back and forth across the map just as she did.

Whisper Chant

Use this chant to help children remember to turn the volume down on their voices.

When we talk in voices LOUD

Two of us sound like a crowd.

It's hard to think, it's hard to hear.

All that noise can hurt your ear!

But, when we whisper, soft as mice,

Then the room feels very nice.

So whisper, whisper, every one,

And we will have some quiet fun.

Turtle Race

Turtles are very s-l-o-w movers. The object of this race is to get around the circle as slowly as possible. Invite children to get down on their hands and knees and see how long they can take to crawl all the way around the circle. You might want to clap, very slowly, for them to "march" to.

Hibernation

Have a circle discussion about the way many animals sleep all winter long. Explain that this is called "hibernation." Name some animals that hibernate and invite children to choose one and pretend to be that animal as it gets ready to hibernate. First, they eat lots and lots. Then they find a cozy spot and curl up. At last, they sleep all winter long, until the spring warmth wakes them.

Extension: Once all the children are "hibernating," read them a soothing story from the Quiet Books list on the next page.

This is a good circle activity, but it also works very well as a lead-in to nap time.

Quiet Books for Peaceful Moments

Here are books to share with your students when they, and you, are ready for a little quiet time.

Te Amo Bebé, Little One by Lisa Wheeler and Maribel Suárez
(Little, Brown and Company, 2004)

Snoozers: 7 Short Short Stories for Lively Little Kids by Sandra Boynton
(Little Simon, 1997)

The Very Quiet Cricket by Eric Carle (Grosset and Dunlap, 1997)

Hush Little Alien by Daniel Kirk (Hyperion, 2001)

Fireflies by Julie Brinckloe (Aladdin, 1986)

The Peace Book by Todd Parr (Little Brown and Company 2004)

Owl Moon by Jane Yolen and John Schoenherr (Philomel Books, 1987)

This Quiet Lady by Charlotte Zolotow (HarperTrophy, 2000)

Ghost Wings by Barbara M. Joosse and Giselle Potter (Chronicle Books 2001)

Down in the Woods at Sleepytime by Carole Lexa Schaefer (Candlewick 2000)

The Lotus Seed by Sherry Garland and Tutsuro Kiuchi (Voyager Books, 1997)

A Quiet Place by Douglas Wood (Simon & Schuster Children's Publishing, 2001)

In the Small, Small Night by Jane Kurtz and Rachel Isadora
(Greenwillow Books, 2005)

Bad Weather, Good Day

When the weather makes it impossible to go outside, you can still have a good day indoors by doing some or all of these circle time activities.

 ## Circle Yoga

To help children get calm and relaxed, teach them some simple yoga postures, such as the following:

Bird: Stand on tiptoe. Lean forward with arms back and fingers spread apart.

Frog: Squat with arms curved over head. Hop and croak.

Snake: Lie on tummy, hands under chest, push up, and arch back.

Cat: Get down on hands and knees. Look down and hump back up, then look up and arch back.

Elephant: Stand on one leg. Reach back and hold onto other foot. Extend other arm out and wave for trunk.

 ## Animal Follow the Leader

Invite children to choose one of the yoga animals, or any others that they like, and lead the group around the circle, with everyone moving like that animal. Change leaders each time around.

 ## Hula Hoop™ Ring Around the Rosey

Instead of holding hands to do "Ring Around the Rosey" get a large Hula Hoop™ and have everyone hold onto it.

Extension: Instead of a Hula Hoop™, use a parachute or round tablecloth.

Imagination Nature Walk Guided Imagery

When it's too awful to go outside, and everyone is feeling antsy, try this. At circle time, ask the children to lie on their backs. Turn the lights down low and read the following guided imagery, pausing where indicated:

Imagination Nature Walk

Is everyone comfortable? Good. Now, we're going to go for a walk in our minds. But first, we want to relax our bodies. First, relax your toes . . . good. Now, relax your legs and knees . . . relax your tummy . . . relax your back . . . relax your hands . . . relax your arms . . . relax your neck . . . relax your face . . . good. Now, imagine that you are standing in front of a door. You open the door and see that it is a warm, sunny day. . . . You step out the door and see a path going into some woods . . . You follow the path, and, as you go into the trees, you see that there are lots of sweet-smelling flowers blooming in the woods. Lean down and smell one of the flowers . . . Now you hear birds singing. You look up. There's a beautiful bird in the tree above you. Listen to its song . . . You start to walk again. You hear someone calling your name. You see a friend coming toward you. You are very happy to see your friend and your friend is happy to see you. . . .You go farther into the woods together. You see a big patch of ripe berries. Pick some and taste them. . . . M-m-m-m. There are lots of butterflies and the air is warm and you are happy. You and your friend talk and laugh and play . . .

It's getting late. It's time to go home. You and your friend walk to the edge of the woods together and say good-bye . . . You walk back on the path to the door you came out of . . . You go in the door . . . You are back in the circle. When you are ready, open your eyes.

Extension: Go around the circle and have students tell about their imaginary nature walk.

Earmuff and Mitten Relay

This is a good winter relay. Show everyone a pair of earmuffs and some mittens. Explain that the object of the relay is to put on the mittens, then the earmuffs, as quickly as possible without any help, then take them off and pass them to the next person, who does the same thing. Use a stopwatch to see how quickly they can get all the way around the circle. You can also do this with a hat, scarf, or other outdoor wear. It's a good way to practice dressing skills.

Giraffe Game

Explain that giraffes don't have any vocal cords, so they are very, very quiet animals. Challenge students to see who can be the best "giraffe" and keep from talking the longest.

Extension: Before playing the game, teach some simple sign language gestures to your class. Challenge them to have a giraffe conversation, using only sign language.

Snake Glide

Everyone stands on the circle, with some space between each child. This is the "tall grass." Invite one child to be the "snake," get down on her tummy (or hands and knees if tummy is too difficult), and weave in and out through the other children as they sing. When the "snake" gets back to her place, she stands up and the next child becomes the snake. Sing the song to the tune of "Pop Goes the Weasel."

Glide in and out of tall grass,
Glide in and out of tall grass,
Glide in and out of tall grass,
Just like a slippery snake.

Extension: Encourage the children in the circle to wave their arms like grass in the wind.

---

92   1-57029-526-3 *Social Development Activities for Circle Time*
Getting Along

 # Quiet CountDown

To get the volume turned down, begin circle time with a quiet countdown. Say, "Ten" very loud, then get softer and softer as you countdown, until *one* is so quiet you can hardly hear it. Invite children to count down with you several times, to practice counting and also to practice quieting down.

Extension: Instead of a countdown, recite the alphabet, starting loud and getting quieter as you go.

 # Big Top

Sew several sheets together (ask parents to donate used sheets) to make a piece of fabric big enough to use for a big top tent for your circle. Sew a loop in the middle of the tent and suspend it from a ceiling hook in the middle of the circle area. Use chairs around the perimeter of the circle to support the sides. Use this as a story tent, a free play area, or a center for a circus play unit.

 # Fairy Ring

Legend claims that fairies dance inside a ring of mushrooms. Make a fairy ring for your classroom by putting open umbrellas around the perimeter of the circle. Play some light, airy, music and have a merry dance.

Extension: Get or make some fairy wings for children to wear when dancing in the fairy ring.

 # Circle Obstacle Course

Place eight to ten various items, such as a beanbag to jump on, a small stuffed animal to jump over, some blocks for stepping-stones, etc., around the edge of the circle. Invite students to take turns running the circle obstacle course.

Extensions: Time children as they take turns running the obstacle course.

After everyone has gone around once, make a new course and do it again.

Do an outdoor circle obstacle course and invite students to ride tricycles around it.

Use stick horses and do a circle barrel race by putting chairs or other large objects that they have to weave in and out of.

 # Animal Pile

If you can't go out to play in the fall leaves, try this, instead. Pile all the stuffed animals, pillows, and any other soft items in the classroom, in the middle of the circle. Invite children to take turns jumping into the pile, just like they would a pile of leaves.

 # Mouse Hunt

Use a toy mouse or other small, stuffed animal. Ask everyone to sit on the circle and close their eyes. Hide the mouse somewhere not too obvious, but still in plain sight. Sit on the circle and say, "One, two, three, go." Everyone searches for the mouse with their eyes only. When they see it, they don't say anything, they just sit back down on the circle. When everyone is back in the circle, or has given up, the first child who spotted the mouse gets to hide it.

Taking Peace Home

Expand your circle of peace by giving your students some good ideas, such as these, to take home with them.

Peace Awards

Notice and jot down when one of your students exhibits peaceful behavior. Make a point of catching everyone being peaceful at least once. Cut 3-inch circles out of cardboard, one for each student and spray them gold. Write each student's name and their peaceful behavior on these "medals." Punch a hole in the top and hang them from ribbons. At the end of the year, have an awards ceremony circle and give out the medals for students to take home.

Extension: If you prefer, you can use gold canning seals for the medals and hot glue the ribbons onto them, which is a bit faster. Use an indelible marker to write on the lids.

"We Are Peaceful" Song

(Sing to the tune of "Hark the Herald Angels Sing.")
Teach this song to your students and encourage them to teach it to their families.

We are peaceful in our hearts

Because we know that's where peace starts.

If I am a friend to you

I hope that you'll be my friend, too.

When with kindness we can play,

We've done our part for peace today.

Peace Doves

Doves are sometimes a symbol of peace. Use the reproducible on page 96 and make a dove for each student to color and cut out. Trace around students' hands and cut out the handprints. Show students how to glue their handprints on the back of the dove for wings. At circle time, go around and ask each child to think of one thing he or she could do to be a peace dove at home. Write what they say on their angels.

Peace Dove Reproducible

Color the dove and cut it out. Make handprint wings to glue to the back.

To be a Peace Dove,

_____

will

_____